CW00392411

Religion—The Weapon of Mass Destruction.

Written by David Kimmeran Aleman

26,257 words

03/05/2023

Photography and Poetry property of David Kimmcran Aleman

- **T**he Reasons

If you look at every war and conflict in the world today apart from the usual greed of overpowered and overpowering egotistical political idiots, the constant and overwhelming subject in the headlights is Religion.

We are in our third year of worldwide pandemic. Covid-19 has claimed the lives of approximately 6 million worldwide. As I start writing this piece of work Vladimir Putin and his Russian boy band are threatening to invade the Ukraine. Boris Johnson is never going to win Prime Minister of the decade, year or indeed moment and above all of this Prince Andrew has made a huge donation to charity out of the kindness of his own heart, if not his own pocket or morality.

The world is crazy, the world is without a shadow of a doubt a time bomb just waiting to explode.

You are only famous and wealthy if you have a sex video of yourself "leaked" to the public. Men have to have a six-pack, tight trousers and no socks whilst girls have fake eyebrows, fake lips and fake intentions. Fake boobs I could live with.

Simply put, and as my old Photography Lecturer Mr. Malcolm Mort told me, "Bad sells!" , Bad news, bad (upsetting or embarrassing) pictures and bad talk, they all sell much better and faster than good, tasteful and honest news."

With that in mind I want to try and look at the connection between good and bad or Religion and Murder. Sounds a bit dramatic you are probably thinking, so hold on.......

This book is my view on religion, my view on politics and my view on the current state of world coherence. I don't claim to know the truth, the whole truth and nothing but the truth, but I know what I believe and more importantly what I don't believe. I haven't just decided to be an atheist, I. like so many others have been hurt by religion, baffled by politicians and sickened by power hungry idiots in designer suits.

Please, therefore, read and enjoy whilst keeping an open mind and an open heart. I dare say nothing I write here will be breaking news to anyone however; I do feel a more logical way of looking at religion needs to be approached. Am I the right person to do that? I don't know. I have no formal training, no real education to speak of and I am not a church going person.

What I have got is an opinion and the world today gives the impression you are not allowed to have an opinion because you are likely to offend someone.

With respect, who cares?

Religion is not about agreeing the person praying next door, it is not about living your life as your neighbouring country does, and religion is not about one entity.
Religion is surely your opinion, your faith and your own belief in the right's and wrongs of living. Is the interpretation that you read into the gospels the same as mine and more importantly does it have to be?

Faith is all about you and your opinion.

I was brought up in a house that was totally committed to God. My mother was a Welsh Baptist and a true and honest believer in her God. I don't know if it was intense belief in all things Holy but as I grew older my disbelief turned to distrust, my distrust turned to anger and then my anger turned to a deep hatred of everything and everyone religious.
Some people say love and hate are two emotions intertwined; no I hate it, all of it. I see religion as the tormentor of my mother, the drainer of all life in my mother and the one thing that she looked for as she was dying, but wasn't there.

In the beginning there was..

Some of the earliest examples of the written word date back almost 5000 BCE. There is evidence there to suggest that a God of some sort was present in the lives of man even back then. Who or what that God was is open to speculation, but I dare say most religions would love to put a claim to it. There are carvings of both humans and animals dating back 38,000 years. There are even zoomorphic (humans with animal features) statues created around this time that suggest and figure crossed between a human and a animal was being worshipped. Around 25,000 years ago there are clear indications of ceremonial burials taking place. Both internment and cremation. These were prominent in Iberia, some parts of Eastern Europe and closer to home, here in Wales .Christians believe that the Earth is no more than perhaps 10,000 years old and of course that it was created in six days by God. That The Garden of Eden was the first place for mankind to stand and that man was Adam. The Bible explains that Adam's partner was Eve, a woman God created from a rib removed from Adam. That all of the beasts therein were friendly and having no embarrassment, Adam and Eve walked around naked. Until that is we are introduced to the Serpent.
Of course we know the serpent is really Satan, The Devil, who then continues to persuade Eve to get Adam to eat an apple from the Tree of Knowledge, something God and forbidden them to do.
The rest as they say is history.....
Or is it?

Religion

The Weapon of mass Destruction

David Kimmeran Aleman

The Body that is there to save the world, is the main body destroying it!

- In the beginning..

Let's start by the mentioning the whole purpose behind my writing. My passion for writing started with poetry and indeed I have written in excess of 500 poems. This doesn't sound a large amount but my poems are normally 10-20 verses long and get changed, re-written and titled differently several times before I am happy with it. the main topic of my writing has always been my lack of trust and belief in anything or anyone religious. I know you are now thinking, "There are many people in the world who don't believe in God, what makes you any different?" Probably nothing, except for the fact I want to believe, in something if not the God we are all taught about.

To the far North West of the Dead sea sit's the sleepy fishing village of Qumran
Between 1946 and 1956 found in caves just outside the village by a herdsman who was looking for a lost sheep, were the now famous Dead Sea scrolls. Dating from 408 BCE

up to 318 CE these scrolls were a day to day account more or less of the life In and around the area.

We are all taught that Jesus, the Messiah in the Christian tradition was born in Bethlehem to Mary and Joseph, who, after travelling from their home 70 miles away by donkey. That he grew up to be the son of a carpenter and at the age of 12 years old started going to the local synagogue to preach the word of his actual father, God. Of course whether you believe this or not is entirely up to you but there are facts that suggest this was all a made up story.

The Dead Sea Scrolls were found in the caves above Qumran and ever since the Christian world has revered and displayed them, even though they strongly suggest the character we know as Jesus Christ was anything but a Messiah.

It has been claimed for centuries that the Jewish religion have always sought to have a 'Peshar', a Messiah. They have always needed for there to be a figurehead to focus all of their religious energy into.

Historical experts from any religious background agree there was a man called Jesus who went on his telling people to love God and each other–this fact is not disputed. However this is where the Dead Sea Scrolls comes into play. Far from being born in Bethlehem, Jesus was born in Qumran to a family of fishermen, not a carpenter's son at all. He would have grown up fishing in the Dead Sea with his father and to live they would sell the fish to others living around them.

Born in the first century AD Jewish historian and politician turned soldier, Flavius Josephus provided us with an accurate documented account of the days in Roman occupied Palestine. He was appointed general of all Jewish forces at the age of 29 and eventually captured by Roman General Vespasian. Rather then stand his ground Josephus capitulated and joined forces with the Roman general. Jospehus was an eyewitness to the destruction of the city of Jerusalem and that of the second Temple in 70 AD. After a while he retired into life in Rome where he started writing his account of the world as he saw it then thus leaving us the account we have today written in words from that actual time.

Over time it has puzzled historical experts as to whether or not the Essene actually wrote the Dead Sea Scrolls and if they were the actual inhabitants of Qumran where the Scrolls were found. The other burning question is whether or not the Jesus mentioned in the scrolls is the same biblical Jesus talked about in the bible? At the time there were three groups who today we might call extremists but then were the community voices depending on where you lived. They were the 'Pharisees, the Sadducee's and the more volatile group, the Essene's. Why volatile?

The Essene's like the other group travelled around preaching love and understanding for all, except if you were Roman, then the Essene's were more than willing to use violence and worse if they thought it necessary. There was a group of Essene's who called themselves the 'Twelve Apostles', they were led at the time by 'Simon and Judas'–later to be known by the Old Testament names Simon Peter and Judas Iscariot. The man we know as Jesus was born as I said earlier into a family of fishermen and when not working his spare time was preaching peace and love. He very soon caught the attention of Judas and soon became firm friends, so much so that along with Simon and Judas, Jesus was soon leading the 'Twelve Apostles'.

The Essene's believed no one should have any possessions and all wealth should be equally shared. All schools should give education freely and willingly no matter who or where you are from. They believed in all things good, true and what would be considered holy. Unfortunately, if someone from a different sect got in the way then they were disposed of.

Due to the methods used by the group they very soon became a focal point for the local Roman soldiers stationed in and around the town. Even though the scrolls are comprised of both the Hebrew Testament (Old Bible) and local sectarian writings, the theme is very much the same in both. That Jesus and the twelve were actually considered to be almost as we would call them today, anarchists. Written both in Hebrew and Aramaic the scrolls definitely give a very differing version of the group compared to the one written in the traditional bible as we know it.

The group including Jesus, Simon-Peter and Judas were becoming more and more prominent in the community and so Roman leaders were now asking questions. Very soon, and even though he was a pacifist Jesus was arrested alongside Simon and Judas as the leaders of this troublesome group.

It is suggested that the Jesus mentioned here and in the scrolls actually had nothing to do with the religious stories, especially as 'John the Baptist ' who is known to have lived in the wilderness close to Qumran is never mentioned in the Dead Sea scrolls. Nevertheless there are similarities between the stories surrounding both groups. In the bible book of Isaiah chapters 35 and 61 there is a list of miracles. These are mentioned in both Luke's writings and in the 'Messianic Apocalypse' written approx. 150 years before. The 'Messianic Apocalypse' appears in the Dead Sea Scrolls and even though the two lists of miracles are not identical they can be measured against each other.

So here we have two men who could be the same individual, we have names of other people surrounding him which are very similar, he grew up the son of a carpenter and most importantly he is a man preaching the ways of love and peace for all. We know that the Jesus in the bible travelled around with his disciples preaching, performing miracles and above all annoying the San Heddrin, the Romans and confusing movie goers for years to come. We know alongside two other criminals he was crucified on Golgotha at the age of thirty-three.

Jesus from Qumran grew up as the son of a fisherman, also joined a group of preachers known as 'the Twelve Apostles', we have learned that due to Judas Iscariot's need for preaching peace with violence the group were arrested and the three ringleaders, Jesus, Simon and Judas were found guilty of public order offense's and so the they too were crucified. However as much as the Romans tried their best to kill the unlucky people nailed to a cross, it is claimed as it was a Friday, a Holy day, if you were alive after 12 hours you could be removed from the cross. It is claimed this Jesus survived, married Mary Magdalene and had two children. He was then supposed to have travelled throughout Europe preaching . He married again after the death of Mary and finally at the age of sixty he settled in Rome, where two years later he died.

It doesn't matter a great deal which of the two versions you believe and I wouldn't be shocked to find there are probably many more stories about Jesus, however as I said earlier the man did live and breath.

So back to today, I am still struggling with depression and still fighting day to day to just get up, get dressed and live.

As a child growing up I learned the entire catalogue of the usual Bible stories word for word neither understanding or indeed caring what they were meant to signify. I knew about Adam and Noah, about Isaac and the burning bush talking to Moses and of course the birth, life and death of Jesus. There are many ways of reading and trying to understand these stories and during this work I hope to give my opinion. Why is my opinion going to be any different from all of the other authors who have tried to undermine the bible?

Simply because I am an atheist who wants to believe but the logic that says I can has not yet reached me. So this work includes my take on Religion and its multifaceted explanation into life and living as a Christian, of any faith. As my writings here will show my mother during her life was an avid church goer and a person who totally committed her life to the worship of her God.

As a popular member of her church we were always, as kids, dragged along to various functions, days out and trips arranged by the congregation. One particular event and even though I could only of been around 10 years old was a visit by a Clergyman by the name of Harralan Popov.

Harralan Popov was born in the small Bulgarian village of Krasno Gradishte. Although initially an atheist, Popov became a Christian as a teenager. In 1929 he was accepted as pastor in the Bulgarian Pentecostal Church. Shortly after attending Bible School in London, he married a Swedish woman, Ruth. He returned to Bulgaria before the outbreak of World War II.

In 1948, in the capital city of Sofia, he was arrested on charges of espionage against the state. After eight months in prison, Popov, and other ministers who had been arrested with him, pleaded guilty. Popov was sentenced to 15 years in prison.[1] He spent the next 13 years and two months in prison. He was released on September 25, 1961 and joined his family in Sweden a year later.

After moving to the United States in 1970, Popov founded Evangelism to Communist Lands Inc., now known as Door of Hope International to bring Bibles and relief to people in oppressive countries in 1972. He recorded his testimony and prison experiences in his autobiography Tortured For His Faith: An Epic of Christian Courage and Heroism in Our Day.

Sitting upstairs in Ebenezer Baptist Church in Swansea I along with my brother 3 years my senior, I was convinced the next couple of hours were going to be boring beyond belief.

With Swansea Railway Station at the end of the road and surrounded by warehouses and Fruit sheds, Ebenezer Street wasn't the ideal location for church-going fashion-conscious snobs. The whole area of Dyfatty was run down. Many of the housing in the area had long gone, replaced by areas of rubble, new pubs or as in the case of many of the old theatres in the area, either a Gay Club or Bingo Hall.

As kids we were forced to attend church by my mother but this was the first time I had ever seen the church pews overflowing with people eager to hear Harralan Popov's story. Looking down I could see this small man in a well fitted suit. His spectacles sat neatly on the end of his nose as he exchanged views with the pastor of the church, Dr. Leighton James.

After an opening prayer and introduction from Dr.James, Mr. Popov began to speak. At first his words were quiet and monotone but very soon as he told of his trials and torture his chest grew, his eyes lit up and looking at everyone straight in the eye at once he bellowed his words with conviction, with passion and with meaning. As the paragraph above suggests he told us all about his childhood, of the love for his mother and father and most of all for faith he found as a teenager. He explained about his pastoral following and how he met and fell in love with his future wife whilst studying in London.

Harralan Popov then spoke of the time from 1948 that he spent in prison for charges of espionage against the state. How as a Pentecostal Christian he was regularly beaten and very often the prisoners would go days without any food. He told us in quite vivid detail how on a couple of occasions left without food for some time they would manage to catch one of the many rats that were scurrying around them on a daily basis and with very little thought of what they were eating, they would share the rats raw meat between them.

The whole evening had me glued to this one man's voice. I can't say it had a profound religious effect on me as I grew up not believing in God, that hasn't changed, what it did do was bring home to me the things we as Mankind are willing to do to each other.

In 16 different prisons Popov was constantly terrorised by his KGB captures or the Bulgarian service men they had working for them.

Upon Popov's arrest, his wife Ruth, a Swedish missionary to Bulgaria, was forbidden to leave Bulgaria for her homeland. After four relentless years, through the help of the Swedish government, she finally received permission to leave with her two children, Rhoda and Paul. Back home in Sweden, she received invitations to speak in the Churches that had supported her missionary work in Bulgaria. She spoke about her husband's imprisonment, and other pastors, for their faith. This led to invitations to speak at large conferences where she began educating churches and denominations that although tradition methods of missionary ministry were no longer possible, there still was a way to work behind the Iron Curtain. Ruth Popov refused to give up hope of the eventual release of her husband from prison. She encouraged Christians to organize prayer groups and petitions on his behalf and other imprisoned Christians.

In 1961 Popov was released. After initially joining his family in Sweden he started taking his horrific story around the world preaching about the word of God and the persecution he suffered for it.

In October 1988, during Glasnost, and for the first time in 26 years, Popov was permitted by Bulgarian authorities to visit the church he pastored in Bulgaria. He died the next month on November 14, 1988 in Glendale, California of complications related to cancer.

As Harralan Popov left that night I stood in front of this little old man who wasn't very much taller than me as a young boy and for the first time in my life I held out my hand to shake his. He took my hand in his right hand and placed his left on the side of my face. The texture of skin was worse than sandpaper and the warmth of his smile radiated to every corner of my face. I was honoured to be in the presence of this man.

Now at almost 54 years old all I can think about is the fact that this man, this little man who gave the world a warm glow where ever he went was so badly treated because of his faith in God.

That was number One

Growing up in the 1970's every evening before bed we sat as a family to watch the news on TV. There was no SKY or Virgin then so it was BBC or ITV or nothing. Living in Swansea every other program was in Welsh so the choice was cut even further.

The usual reporters appeared before us to tell us of a Government bore calling another Government bore names, or how a film star had died or how the weather was going yet again to be terrible. Frequently however we were also told of the Troubles as they were called in Northern Ireland and how in the Middle East yet another British Missionary had been kidnapped by one of the many religious factions that were running rife.

One such man was Terry Waite, looking at this man who, with his big eyes, very tall stature and big bushy beard, he was bound to stand out in any crowd.

Waite was the Assistant for Anglican Communion Affairs for the then Archbishop of Canterbury, Robert Runcie, in the 1980s. As an envoy for the Church of England, he travelled to Lebanon to try to secure the release of four hostages, including the journalist John McCarthy. He was himself kidnapped and held captive from 1987 to 1991.

Very often on the news a reporter would stand in front of Westminster Abbey for effect and tell us all how an envoy had been sent to attempt to free the British hostages being held. Very soon the ongoing saga of Waite's imprisonment would be mentioned almost every night. He spent a total of 1763 days in captivity with approximately 1460 in solitary confinement.

Terry Waite had successfully talked his way through many hostage release scenarios but his ongoing friendship with American Colonel Oliver North and his use of American Military transport made the group I.J.O. Islamic Jihad Organisation see Waite as a valuable asset and bargaining tool.

So on the news night after night we would be shown old footage of this larger than life man standing alongside Robert Runcie the then Archbishop of Canterbury dwarfing him in comparison.

Years later in 1997 I think, Terry Waite was speaking about his experiences at several meetings around the religious groups of Swansea University. After one such meeting he came for dinner with friends to the Restaurant I worked in at the time. After everyone had left and for all intense purposes we had finished work we sat for a short while talking to Waite. I was shocked to see this man who obviously with his great height and become a slight reflection physically of the man I used to see on TV. He told us all about his experiences at the hands of the I.J.O. and how he felt towards the men who individually hurt him so much.

So once again as with Harralan Popov a man who has given his life to his belief in goodness, in doing what is right and his God is treated so badly

Then I think the worst:

From all religions and walks of life there has always been the need to publicly show your strength and non-wavering commitment to whatever God you believe in.

During my life time I can recall many news reports and hearsay stories of people being executed for just not following a religion. Then as we came into the age of the internet and global news all of sudden we began to get graphic videos emerging on the world wide web showing missionaries, aid workers or military personnel publicly flogged, paraded and at its worst filmed having their heads cut off.

Two high profile examples of this were Alan Jenning and David Haines.

Alan Henning (15 August 1967 – c. 3 October 2014) was an English taxicab driver-turned-volunteer humanitarian aid worker. He was the fourth Western hostage killed by Islamic State of Iraq and the Levant (ISIL) whose killing was publicised in a beheading video. Henning was captured during ISIL's occupation of the Syrian city of Al-Darna.

David Cawthorne Haines (9 May 1970 – c. 13 September 2014) was a British aid worker who was captured by the Islamic State of Iraq and the Levant (ISIL) in early 2013 and beheaded in early September 2014. Isil were so proud to show the world how barbaric they could be. How strong and powerful they were.
Yet all they had actually done is capture two men who were there to do good, honest and humanitarian work. These men were not professional soldiers, they were not men who could fight their way out of trouble with skills learned after years in the military, they were honest hard working men who just wanted to do some good in the world.

So what did they in fact achieve? Apart from decimating two families home here in the U.K.

Absolutely nothing.

Why did they do it?

They did it to show strength, to tell the world that the God they believe in, their religion, their law is the true law, true God and only worthy religion.

So all I can say is if God in any guise could see all of this happening in his/her, it's name surely it would all be stopped?

I recently heard two quotes which hit home to me with some resonance. The First is as follows:

"I feel like I am on the other side of a mirror watching the world"

My full name is David Kimmeran Aleman, growing up my family and school friends called me Kim. All through school I was ridiculed, called a girl because I had a girl's name. I wore glasses from the age of four so now I was also "four eyes". I was over weight and had over active bladder which meant I was peeing literally every 10 minutes. All through Junior School I was bullied.

Then at the age of about ten I started to grow and sprout hair everywhere before any of the other kids so my surname in school suddenly changed to Ape-man.

Proactively every day and by clock-work I was set upon, punched, kicked and spat on. All through lessons I was threatened called names and made to feel like I wasn't actually there.

I had a few close friends who in many ways saved me from totally losing the plot. My friend David Harris was always there for me and I would like to think me for him. I can remember one funny story with David, we were on a school trip to Manor Park in Tenby during either the first or second year of Comp. David fell asleep on the bus home whilst holding an apple and we managed to eat the whole apple just leaving the core still in his fingers without waking him.

I felt I didn't belong, I shouldn't be here. I could see everyone else in my peer group as living a totally different life to me. I still feel like that today. Forty years on.

I find it easy to make friends but I can't commit myself to anything, for example if the guys from work are going out for a drink, to watch rugby or Christmas, anything, I always agree to go but I can never actually get myself to turn up

The second quote was from a documentary I watched about young women who in current modern day Syria were systematically raped and kept as sex slaves.

One of the ladies concerned was asked if she wanted justice, do you want your captures executed, as the law there commands?

Her response was:

"You can't cure harm with harm !"

Let me ask you a question?

If you read a book about a young boy who is brought up and finds very quickly that due to his family tree, whichever one you believe, he soon performs miracles, he soon becomes hunted by a group of people who think they are the rightful leaders. Very soon he has become a bit of a local hero and has many followers. Then there are books and films all about him and very soon avid followers who know everything about him, and importantly they are positive he is the chosen one. Do you recognize this partial story and relate it to the story of Jesus Christ?

or....

"One day, will people think Harry Potter is the Messiah?"

The next segment will end this first chapter and it is my personal reasons for disliking everything religious. I was recently asked if I believed in God?

This is my answer.....

At the same moment the Japanese Imperial Empire attacked the American Naval base at Pearl Harbour the world was also delivered of a beautiful baby girl. It was December 1941. My mother Ethel Pauline Ellis was born on the 8th December to Alice and Thomas Ellis. She was the last born of seven children.
Even though I never met her, people told me my Grandmother Alice was the most caring, loving and peaceful person you would ever wish to meet.
My Grandfather, as many men of that time, a time of poverty, insecurity and fear, was a drunken bully.
My mother was born on Cwm Farm a small holding rented by Thomas from the council. To make ends meet and as he had no farming skills he sublet the fields to local farmers. So now he was learning to look after animals, making money and had none of the overheads involved. The house my mother was born in was later used as the stables. It is gone now replaced by a very large Mediterranean style Villa. The fields are now new build family homes.

History gone.
The house was a three storey house built with no running water and electricity only in the bottom room. This was the living, kitchen and entrance room all rolled into one. The first floor was for best and then the top floor was the two large bedrooms. Being the last born my mother was ten years younger than her nearest sibling, her sister Sonia. Also at home was her brother Armyn. Just like their father Armyn was a drunk and a bully. They both had been banned from most of the pubs in the area. Surrounded by the district of Cockett, Cwm Farm was at the bottom of a deep valley surrounded by Oak trees and steep muddy lanes to the main road.
The nearest life was the Asylum at Cefn Coed just above the farm. The main track from the road down to the farm was very steep, very rough and guarded by three heavy

metal gates. They were called the funeral gates so called because they were only opened for a funeral. Only a horse drawn hearse could make it up and down that route. There were no phone boxes, no internet, and no mobiles. Once down the farm you were completely cut off from the rest of the world.

   One of my mother's earliest memories was of a time she had tried to forget, was as a 6/7 year old running up the muddy track, usually barefoot from bed, in the middle of the night, in the pitch black and terrified to try and find a Policeman, anyone on the main road to get some help to her mother. She would eventually return to the farm house the same way down that scary track to return and face whatever punishment given to her mother by either her father, brother or both for not making food in time or for saying something they didn't agree with. The pain this small child had to deal with affected her for the rest of her life.

   As an adult and visiting the farm with my mother many years later she couldn't go near the house. Alice, my Grandmother was raised as a devout Welsh Baptist. My mother followed her in the worship of their god.

Where was God during the beatings?

As a teenager my mother Pauline, got a job at the local Smiths Crisp factory. It was here she met my father Keith Aleman. Of European decent Keith didn't want to settle in Swansea and indeed the dripping tap of sexual adventures which ran constant during the early 1960's he wanted to drink from as often as possible.

Soon after they married and after my brother 3 years later I was born. It was 1968 and my father once again had an itch he needed scratching, he left us all when I was 3 months old. After living away from Swansea for 5 years or so and returning with her tail firmly between her legs with two very young kids in tow it was 1970 and the start of a horrific time for my mother. Returning to Swansea she was shunned. Not only a divorcee, but with no money, no home and two kids she was just going to be a burden to everyone. The only person who did eventually help was her eldest sister Ruby. She was lovely. All my Aunts and Uncles had good jobs, nice homes and plenty of money. My mother had the clothes she stood up in and two babies.

Where is God now?

After a year living with Ruby and her husband Herbert the bullying and threats from Herbert became too much for my mother. After month after month of begging the council gave us a 2 bedroom flat in the Mayhill area of Swansea. 23 Byron Crescent. As with everyone then you only used the back door which led onto a veranda on which was housed our outside toilet. Then there were steps down to the back garden and eventually the road. We weren't allowed near the windows on a Tuesday if we weren't in school as that was the day the Rent man called and we had to hide. My mother had a couple of cash in hand jobs but nothing secure, she was smoking heavily, her health was bad.

When I was 6 it was announced that Byron Crescent was to get a complete facelift. We had the choice of moving into a hostel and then back into the flat when the work was done or move to somewhere new entirely. We moved.

We moved to Creidiol Road, only a mile away but for the first time in my short life we had an inside toilet. Until now I didn't even know toilets could have lights in them. What next could we even get some toilet paper or was that just too farfetched?

After a while her family started to make an effort and pretty soon every Sunday meant a family trek to church. We would sit with Sonia her sister. A church snob. Had to have the best hat, best clothes and had to have special prayer services in her house.

Church had now taken over my mother's life.

Was there really a God?

After my mother's death in 2005 two things shook me. One a memory and one a complete surprise.

The memory.

In 1976 and as an 8 year old all I wanted as with my brother and friends was to see the new film coming out, Star Wars. Nothing like this had been seen before it was a must see for everyone. Not know to me or my brother Yan, my mother for months and months scrimped and saved every penny she could to get us tickets for the film. She was determined she wasn't going to let us down, we weren't going to be left out. She even saved enough for a bus home.

To get home we would catch the bus outside the dentist's in Orchard Street then the bus laden with passengers would struggle its way up Mount Pleasant Hill at a snail's pace until our stop at "Leaker's". Haven't got a clue why we called it that. The bus actually stopped outside Eagan Fish and Chip shop.

My mother had saved for months for cinema tickets, bought sweets and still had enough for a bus home and now my brother and I gave her hell because she couldn't buy us chips. The mile or so walk home from the bus, we whinged, we moaned and we kept on and on. To this day I can see her sitting on the couch breaking her heart because we were so horrible to her.

I didn't remember any of this until after she died.

The surprise

Going through her paperwork after her funeral I found loads of appointment cards for various hospital visits in I think about 1971 or 1972. It was a private hospital. Sonia my Aunt for 37 years was married to Ronald. When they divorced my mother who had again fallen fowl of her family became Ronald's partner. I would often visit him as he was the only link I had with my mother. I asked him all about these hospital visit's and he explained that my mother miss-carried twins heavily into the pregnancy. She never told who the father was but he obviously had money to afford a private hospital. Neither my brother nor I knew anything. How she must of felt. Being abandoned by her husband leading to divorce, being ostracized by most of her own family, being a single mother with no money and now to lose two babies.

Where was God now?

As I grew into my teens and now flatly refusing to go to church and with my brother now living in Germany my mother threw herself totally into her belief in God. In many ways she became obsessed. She was a "Bible Basher".

Every conversation was about God, about forgiveness about Jesus and how he saved us all.

She was going to three services on a Sundy. A prayer meeting Monday night and Wednesday night. Thursday morning was bible class in her sister Sonia's house and on a Friday afternoon another prayer meeting.

As a single parent with poor health, she smoked very heavily which was now affecting her chest functions; she couldn't hold a full time job. The powers that be decided for her to keep her benefits she could however do a 12 hour a week job.

So now she got her perfect job, a cleaner in her church. When she wasn't worshipping in it she was cleaning it.

Very soon she was one of the fixture and fittings of the church and soon she became sucked into the whole fashion parade and one up man ship that grew in the church. As part of this she fell head of heels in love with her Pastor. He was everything. He was married and I think really my mother was just awe struck by him. It wasn't reciprocated. One of the funniest events of this time was my mother's baptism. My brother was home from Germany so we both agreed to go and watch this strange event. As her pastor lowered her backwards into the water my mother panicked and having then took a large mouth full of water coughed violently sending her false teeth flying through the air until they settled floating away from the two of them stood looking in terror at her plastic Gnasher's. Yan and I were sat upstairs directly above the well and couldn't help ourselves from dissolving into a lather of laughter, tears and embarrassment for my mother.

Soon after and with Yan back in Germany in the Army and with me putting more and more pressure on my mother to move house as I was too embarrassed to tell my college friends I lived in Mayhill, she had a complete nervous breakdown.

On her return home her Bible bashing became worse and worse. She was Dot Cotton on Speed. She was constantly quoting the bible and praying and spending all of her spare time in her church.

What was her God doing to her?

Then the worst

My mother Pauline had a very close friend, Lilly. Lilly had terminal cancer and so my mother spent most of her spare time now caring for her at Lilly's home. Sometimes she would stay overnight and even though they both knew the end was near their friendship grew and grew.

One afternoon my mother entered Lilly's to find her solicitor sitting there whilst Lilly amended her will instructing him to sell the house upon her death and make sure my mother was left a comfortable amount of money. My mother had never had money and so even as the thought of losing her friend was painful, Lilly's kindness was overwhelming.

Two days before her death Lilly was visited by her solicitor once again this time accompanied by the Pastor from my mother's church, her hero. Lilly died and very soon the will was to be read.

It transpired that Lilly had left everything including the house to the Pastor my mother received nothing. It was obvious in her dying state he had convinced her to change the will. It also then emerged he was having several affairs with various female parishioners and so very quickly he was hounded out of the church completely breaking my mother's heart.

She had another breakdown, she was devastated.

Where was God now?

Several years and several breakdowns later my mother was smoking very heavily still and was depending on several inhalers a day to survive.

After visiting my mother on December 26th 2004 and watching on TV the terrible events of the Tsunami which killed thousands she told me she had been quite unwell had some tests and the results were going to be ready New Year's Eve. I took her to the hospital. It was confirmed she had Bronchial Carcinoma, Lung Cancer. It was very small, pea size but was sitting against the heart valve in her left lung. It was unlikely to kill her but would make her breathing even more difficult. She wasn't fit enough for any invasive treatment so they would try and help with drugs.

She just gave up.

Can you see her God?

As the weeks past as long as she had her fags, her coffee and the odd cheese sandwich she was happy. Her weight dropped dramatically, her strength disappeared and she grew paler by the day. From being an active 63 year old she suddenly became a little old lady.

Come on God do something!

Two days before my Daughter Olivia's 4th birthday Ronald phoned me to tell me to come down to Swansea as he was really worried about my mother. When I got there I called an ambulance and she was rushed to Singleton Hospital. The staff there was amazing I have to say.
They probed, poked and prodded and eventually said her oxygen levels were dangerously low. They put her on a mask and said give her 48 hours and she should be home. That was a Saturday. Sunday she seemed a little better and late in the day I was told that Pneumonia had settled in her right lung. By the Monday afternoon she was in a coma.
They kept her comfortable with drugs and oxygen through the week and then on the Friday I was told that nothing more could be done and it was only a matter of time. They stopped all treatment. By now different members of her church were coming into her hospital room and sitting around her either praying or reading from the bible. I hated it. It was the end of the football season and there was football constantly on the TV so every time one of her church buddies came in I made sure the football was on full volume.
       During the evening of Saturday 30th April for the first time in a week she opened her beautiful crystal blue eyes and a single tear flowed like a Tsunami down her cheek. I broke down and cried for hours.

She was looking for her God

I was shattered and alone.

The next day on my last legs I knew I had to go home, shower and eat and sleep. Not wanting to disturb anyone I slept on the sofa downstairs. At half past midnight the hospital phoned and asked me to attend. Nothing more was said. The 48 mile drive to the hospital was terrible. I was alone, scared and tired.

I entered her room terrified but when I saw her she looked beautiful, peaceful and pain free. She was dead.

The nurse asked me to remove her jewellery and watch and explained what happened next. The nurse was obviously heavily pregnant and so I felt really bad that she should be doing this.

I hugged my mother, I kissed her and I told her I would always love her. I told her Olivia would always know of her and I would always talk about her to Olivia.

Where was her God now?

So do I believe in God?

A person, my mother gives her life to him but he is nowhere to be seen

There is so much death in the world in his name

How can such a selfish, uncaring and arrogant entity exist?

Thus started my religious investigations, my research and most of all my distrust in everything to do with a God that likes death as much as anything else. It got so much at one point I felt physically sick just entering a church.

We are currently in the midst of real turmoil as Vladimir Putin's Russian army has invaded neighbouring Ukraine. With this in mind and even though I will continue to explain my religious views from time to time I will just insert a paragraph or two similar to diary pages.

Diary 1

It has been five weeks since Putin's Russian soldiers invaded Ukraine. Some of the images we get to see on the news are horrific at best an absolute disgrace at any other level.

When will the so called 'leaders' of the world realise that they are in power to serve the communities around them? Okay so the likes of Putin and other oppressive rulers were not 'fairly' voted in rather took the vote, but here in the UK, in USA and in many main-land European countries the figureheads at the helm of government are silver spooned, multi-millionaires with buckets full of cash and degrees from university but absolutely no shred of common sense or empathy. Now the invasion of Ukraine is wrong on so many levels with as of todays news an estimated 15000 Russian soldiers alone have been killed, that's without the estimated 1000+ civilian deaths, however, closer to home how many people in the UK are now going to die because of the price hikes on fuel bills?

Not the same I know but why isn't our Prime Minister and his hoard of idiots doing something about it? The people of Ukraine have had no choice in what is happening, as with every other war going on, but here in the 'First World', yeh right? Here in the UK surely our political leaders can do much, much more to help those who are going to face fuel poverty, those who will be making a choice to eat or not, to stay warm or not? There may not be guns and rockets killing people here but for me those dying or assured to die are doing so because of ignorance and selfish lifestyles by those supposed to be helping.

Get rid of the silver spoon brigade and get someone real into Downing Street.

- Religion and the Nazi's

The largest Religious 'Business' in the world for many, many years has been the Roman Catholic Church. It is also one of the biggest money-makers in the world. As the smallest city in the world, the Vatican City is richer than most countries. The Sistine Chapel ceiling is insured for $6.4 million alone.

Born on April 20th 1889 to parents Alois Hitler and Klara Polzl, Adolf Hitler was an Austrian-Hungarian citizen most of his life before becoming the leader of Germany in 1933. He lived near Linz and later on studied art in Vienna before moving to Germany where he joined the army earning the Iron Cross for bravery after being blinded in a gas attack whilst carrying information from the front line to his superiors. Much is known about Hitler thanks to diaries kept at the time, news reporting and of course the instigation of the Second World War. Much is written about the Nazi's and the extermination of six million Jewish people in the many horrendous death camps around Poland and Germany, what is not more commonly known is the strong relationship the Nazi party had with the Roman Catholic Church.

One of the things I have always had conflict with is the Christian ability to forgive. The bible tells you that no matter what another person does to you, you must offer forgiveness and forget everything that has gone before.

But I can't help thinking where is the line drawn? Is there a limit to which a Christian work's? Once he or she has been wronged three times they cannot forgive again? I agree holding on to the pain someone else has caused you for too long can be destructive. Surely that is just human emotion and common sense?

So with this in mind, do we forgive those who bomb our cities? Do we say "Hey, it's OK, I forgive you "? I just can't get my head around it.

The Christian, and I say Christian just for explanation I know that there are many and varied religious teachings and followers, the religious follower then, their ability to just accept atrocities and put it down to the Devil and just carry on baffles me. As a true believer in God, whatever your calling may be, you are taught to accept everyone, well that doesn't happen for one. You are encouraged to help everyone, treat everyone as equals, to be tolerant and caring. To preserve and worship life.

As a Christian would you forgive someone like Hitler for his war crimes? Where do you draw the line?

I know I am being dramatic and argumentative, but I am trying to understand.

In the bible it says:

But in Matthew (5:38-42) in the New Testament, Jesus repudiates even that notion. "Ye have heard that it hath been said, An eye for an eye, and a tooth for a tooth: But I say unto you, That ye resist not evil: but whosoever shall smite thee on thy right cheek, turn to him the other also

Does this mean it was wrong to execute these people?

Misguided?

Revenge

Proverbs 20:22

Do not say, "I'll pay you back for this wrong!" Wait for the LORD, and he will avenge you.

After the war many people who had endured and survived the horrific days spent in the German Concentration Camps went on to become once again successful people. Perhaps not in a materialistic way, but they made homes, had families and grew to build a future for those around them, many living until their 90's or more. Vengeance is something bible says we should never succumb to. If someone murder's a member of your family and you are a devout Christian who then goes and kills the killer?

Are they still a Christian?

Is the executioner who carries out his job with empathy and even sympathy, is he clear of all sin for doing so?

From the Nazi commanders of WW2 to Saddam Hussein and Colonel Gaddaffi. Even centuries before these examples people have been executed for breaking the law. In early times people could be hung for just stealing an apple for food. Death has no religious bias.

I have mentioned the Inquisitions and spoken about the people killed for being witches, but the people who did the killing or the executions can they consider themselves without sin? Or does the fact that many years ago people were ignorant about the truth. People only knew what the Bible bashers told them. I am trying to understand. If God is real, if sin is an actual 'thing' if I kill someone for being a killer does this absolve me of the sin of killing?

A fact that was held as a secret for many years by the American Army that uncovered it was that after the war there was an undercover group of Jewish fighters calling themselves "The Avengers" who were set in killing as many Germans as possible.

The Nokmim (Hebrew: הנוקמים), also referred to as The Avengers or the Jewish Avengers, were a Jewish partisan militia, formed by Abba Kovner and his lieutenants Vitka

Kempner and RozkaKorczak from the surviving remnants of the United Partisan Organization (Fareynikte Partizaner Organizatsye), which operated in Lithuania under Soviet command.

Kovner wanted to kill men, women and children, he didn't care if they were innocent of any crimes carried out by the army, and they were Germans. The group wanted to kill 6million Germans, the number of Jewish people killed by the Holocaust. Unfortunately for them when the ship they were travelling on was nearing Toulon in France the British Soldiers on board noticed their papers were forged. Before being caught they threw all of the poison overboard, so plan B kicked in.

The plan was to poison the water supplies of major cities, Berlin, Nuremburg, and Munich. On a smaller scale in a plan which was apparently agreed upon by the Israeli President Chaim Weissemen, was to poison 3000 loaves of bread with arsenic that was to be served to SS Officers that were being held after the war in Stalag 13, an American Prisoner of War Camp

Out of the 4000 inmates at the camp some 2300 were affected with varying levels of sickness and about 400 SS soldiers actually dying, however this has been refuted with no actual proof of any deaths having been recorded.

So nowhere near the levels of death they wanted or set out to achieve but still 400 murders in the name of revenge.

Does this act alongside many other probable unknown murders by the group make them justified in their actions? Does it make them criminals or givers of justice?

I know and agree that many of the points I make probably the rants of an atheistic middle aged man but, I am trying to explain, I am attempting to argue that we do not need to believe in an entity that I believe, does not exist.

The Jews were persecuted for being Jewish - a religion

The Catholics murdered people who didn't conform to their – religion

Islamic State murder because they believe they are justified due to – their religion Closer to home in Northern Ireland the Catholics fought with Protestants – both religions Years ago people were burned or crucified or fed to a hungry lion because the God or Idol they worshipped wasn't the same as their captures.

Everyone one of us on this planet has a heart, a brain and lungs and everything that puts us together to make this blob we call humanity. There is not one man or woman on this planet that is better at being a human than the person next to them.

My best friend Simon has a step-son who has Cerebral palsy, does this lesson him as a man, no, he has a wicked sense of humour, he is always looking for the care workers who call because they are mostly pretty young girls that get his heartbeat racing. Does the fact that he cannot learn as others and absorb information as others can do stop him from believing in God? On the day of judgement, if there is ever to be one, would every human being in the world today with a learning difficulty, Who is unable to follow any sort of faith, would they be turned away from God?

To believe in any God, whatever faith you have to accept without question or hesitation the stories you are being told.

For me I need proof.

I know my doctor fixed a problem with a broken disc in my back because I was able to feel the after effects. I felt the nervousness before the operation and the needle being stuck in my hand. I felt the pain that the next 3 months of rehabilitation took. I know even after the blitz many parts of Swansea were flattened and rebuilt because I can see it with my own two eyes.

I know and even though she worshipped her God with all of her heart, I know my mother died in pain of lung cancer and pneumonia.

I know because I can see, I can hear and I can feel.

In the Franco Zefferelli epic "Jesus of Nazareth", Jesus played by Robert Powell is approached by a Roman Centurion played by the late Ernest Bourgnine. The Centurion explains to Jesus that he has a slave at home who he thinks of more as a son who has become gravely ill. He asks Jesus to help the slave. Jesus asks the Roman to take him to his house, the Centurion replies that he wouldn't like Jesus to go to his home as he is not worthy, and that he doesn't have to see Jesus save the slave he just has to know that Jesus has said it is done, that would be enough.

Jesus replied that he had rarely seen such faith and that because of this faith the slave the Centurion loved as a son was now saved.

So let's look at this in detail;

A Roman Centurion would almost certainly be put to death for what would probably considered as fraternizing with the enemy, no way would it happen.

A Roman Soldier befriends a slave? Slaves were nearly always either Jews or another nationality brought to them from other battles or raids. A Roman soldier would never have consorted in any way favourably with anyone not Roman.

Then a Roman soldier who believes and follows Pagan Gods, as he would have done all of his life, suddenly accepts the fact that by just saying so a man can cure his slave, whilst not even being in the same place, he accepts and believes that this not only will but has happened.

If I told you Aliens had just landed a massive space ship on the roof of Buckingham Palace what would be the first thing you would do?

First of all you would mock me and probably try and get me sectioned under the mental health act. Next you would if you had any thoughts at all it could be real, you would turn on your television or radio or whatever communication devise you are using to see it, to hear it or to feel the anticipation. You would want proof.

So back to the Nazi's, the Pope at the time was Pope Pius XII. Born March 2nd 1876, Eugenio Maria Giuseppe Giovanni Pacelli was head of the Roman Catholic Church and considered 'The Vicar of Christ' between 1939 up until his death in October 1958. One of the biggest fears he had was the strength that Communist Russia was showing at the borders of Europe. The Pope considered as the Nazi Party was also against the Communist's then they must be a good group to be in bed with, so to speak.

Before becoming Pope, Cardinal Pacelli worked as Vatican representative in Germany. His relationship with the Nazi leaders has been heavily looked upon with anger and disdain, yet, he did in fact encourage many Churches to give aid to Jews in Germany. However, it was well known that the Nazi leaders began to think Pius to be an Allied Forces sympathizer and indeed the Allied leaders considered Pope Pius did very little either to condemn the Holocaust or to try and stop it. In the end Germany stopped speaking to the Pope as they couldn't accept his 'non neutrality' as was common for Vatican City residents. Of course the Vatican is in Rome, Rome being the capital of Italy and Italy being German allies meant the threat of bombing or more from the British and American forces meant the Pope had to back track and distance himself from the German Reich as quickly as possible.

I can remember sitting in bar in the then West Berlin with my Dad, I think it was 1982 or around that time. We started talking to an elderly man in the corner of the bar. It turned out he was 97 years old and had served in the army for most of his adult life. As he was from a farming background he was used mainly in the production side of feeding the soldiers on the front line when possible. He explained he served under the Kaiser, under Brandenburg and then of course under the Nazi's. He claimed and we had no reason to doubt him, that he and his group of friends had no idea of the Holocaust as it was happening and that as soldiers they were just following orders laid down. As a German, sorry, a proud and Christian German he did what his duty demanded but not to the extent of murder. He fully admitted if a soldier from an opposing army stood before him he would have killed rather than be killed as his commanders demanded, but to kill a complete innocent because of their Faith is something he would not have done.

You can tune into all sorts of media channels on tv and at some point a documentary explaining that Adolf Hitler didn't in fact die in the bunker back in 1945 but was in fact secreted out via vast tunnels, that an airplane took off from the centre of town delivering him to Norway where he boarded first a ship and then a submarine that 3 months later deposited him in Argentina. That is a subject for a different book and indeed has been written about several times.

The Rat Lines - Many high-ranking fascists and Nazis who escaped Europe via the ratlines after World War II included.: Ante Pavelić, Adolf Eichmann and Josef Mengele. Even though it is said Hitler escaped via Norway most of the Nazi and fascist wanted escaped via various routes through Spain and Italy then by sea again as Hitler, to South America.

Pryor to the war Argentina had a close relationship with the Vatican due to the many different forms of Catholicism in South America. As we have already noted Pope Pius before the war was the Vatican representative in Germany and was indeed in close contact with the Nazi party.

The origins of the first ratlines are connected to various developments in Vatican–Argentine relations before and during World War II. As early as 1942, Monsignor Luigi Maglione contacted Ambassador Llobet, inquiring as to the "willingness of the government of the Argentine Republic to apply its immigration law generously, in order to encourage at the opportune moment European Catholic immigrants to seek the necessary land and capital in our country". Afterwards, a German priest, Anton Weber, the head of the Rome-based Society of Saint Raphael, travelled to Portugal, continuing to Argentina, to lay the groundwork for future Catholic immigration; this was to be a route which fascist exiles would exploit. According to historian Michael Phayer, "this was the innocent origin of what would become the Vatican ratline".

Spain, not Rome, was the "first centre of ratline activity that facilitated the escape of Nazi fascists," although the exodus itself was planned within the Vatican. Among the primary organizers were Charles Lescat, a French member of Action Française – an organization suppressed by Pope Pius XI and rehabilitated by Pope Pius XII – and Pierre Daye, a Belgian with contacts in the Spanish government. Lescat and Daye were the first to flee Europe with the help of Argentine cardinal Antonio Caggiano.

By 1946, there were hundreds of war criminals in Spain, and thousands of former Nazis and fascists. According to then–United States Secretary of State James F. Byrnes, Vatican cooperation in turning over these "asylum-seekers" was "negligible". Phayer claims that Pius XII "preferred to see fascist war criminals on board ships sailing to the New World rather than seeing them rotting in POW camps in zonal Germany". Unlike the Vatican emigration operation in Italy that centred on Vatican City, the ratlines of Spain, although "fostered by the Vatican," were relatively independent of the hierarchy of the Vatican Emigration Bureau.

To critics, the pontiff's refusal to publicly condemn the Nazis represents a shameful moral failing with devastating consequences. In his polarizing 1999 biography of Pius, British journalist John Cornwell argued that the religious leader placed the papacy's supremacy above the plight of Europe's Jews, winning a modicum of power—and protection from the rising threat of communism—by becoming "Hitler's pope" and pawn. Supporters, however, say that Pius' silence was calculated to prevent German retaliation and ensure the continued success of the Catholic Church's behind-the-scenes efforts to aid victims of Nazi persecution.

If we look back to the very start of what the world says is the beginning of Christianity, the birth of Christ, we are told all about the logistics of the area, of the nationalities and of course the beliefs. We are told the main Christian faith of the time is Judaism. If therefore as is suggested the Jewish faith is very important why would the leader of the church, the so called 'Vicar of Christ', why would the pope stand my and accept the Nazi treatment of the Jewish race?

If the Pope and his pals did help Nazi Officers escape why haven't they been held responsible? Posthumously or not? After the war and indeed after the Nuremberg Trials as more and more information came to light more and more people were involved in investigating what had gone on. One of the main 'Hunters' if you like of escaped Nazi's was Simon Wiesenthal

Wiesenthal KBE was born 31/12/1908 and died aged 96 on 20/09/2005, he was a Jewish Austrian Holocaust survivor, Nazi hunter, and writer. He studied architecture and was living in Lwów at the outbreak of World War II. He survived the Janowska concentration camp (late 1941 to September 1944), the Kraków-Płaszów concentration camp (September to October 1944), the Gross-Rosen concentration camp, a death march to Chemnitz, Buchenwald, and the Mauthausen-Gusen concentration camp (February to 5 May 1945).

After the war, Wiesenthal dedicated his life to tracking down and gathering information on fugitive Nazi war criminals so that they could be brought to trial. In 1947, he co-founded the Jewish Historical Documentation Centre in Linz, Austria, where he and others gathered information for future war crime trials and aided refugees in their search for lost relatives. He opened the Documentation Centre of the Association of Jewish Victims of the Nazi Regime in Vienna in 1961 and continued to try to locate missing Nazi war criminals. He played a small role in locating Adolf Eichmann, who was captured in Buenos Aires in 1960, and worked closely with the Austrian justice ministry to prepare a dossier on Franz Stangl, who was sentenced to life imprisonment in 1971.

In summary then, the highest religious position, the 'Vicar of Christ', his Holiness Pope Pius XIII was instrumental in the act of turning a blind eye when his people, the Jewish race, Christians were being persecuted for their faith. Murdered for their religion and exterminated for following a faith. How can that be justified? How can it be that a Holy man accepts any murder, of a single person, a group or a race?

I think the simple fact is that I, we can go into all of the stories about escaping Nazi's, we can watch movies, read books and listen to stories, however the simple truth always brings us back to the fact that it was because of religion, because of faith in God that these people were murdered and why their leader turned a blind eye. Yes I hear you shout, the Pope is the leader of the Roman Catholic Church, but if you believe in the biblical stories the first Pope was Simon-Peter who was -Jewish!

"All through this work, apart from my mother and I, I have placed photographs for no other reason than to show the beauty that there actually is in the world"

Diary 2

It is 6 weeks. SIX BLOODY weeks, yet all the British press want to talk about is Prince Harry and Meghan's visit, about who is going to be the next James Bond and of course not forgetting the named, famous and rich idiots that parade through the carpeted corridors of Whitehall.

The future of our country as we all know are our kid's and the work ethic and education we encourage them to welcome. Yet, our brilliant leaders who break the law with parties during lockdown are fined only £50. Just look at the headlines from recent weeks. The Prime Minister, the Chancellor and most of the Boris brigade are millionaires or if not then pretty dam close. £50 is probably what they use to tip the waiter at lunch. Yet for University students living by whatever means they can gather, working evenings to pay the rent and (the odd pint) and leaving with thousands of pounds worth of debt are fined £10,000. Now, ok, yes they broke the law and I have to say if the fine is £10k then great, they deserve it but what is the difference between their parties and those of the Boris brigade? The difference is that it's the Boris Brigade that came up with the rule. So why haven't they been fined £10,000?

Ukraine is still under the continued fist of Putin's Russian military. We are being shown pictures and being told of mass graves, of people being tortured, women being raped and children being buried alive under bombed buildings. So what is our government actually doing?

Boris, fair play has been to the Ukraine. No matter who you are and no matter what kind of security you have it must have been scary for him. I don't agree with his ways but I applaud him for going.

We need to make the transition from war to peace an easier task to achieve. We need to sanction the hell out of Putin and most of all the World needs to stand up to this power mad moron.

Finally, for today when I think the Boris Brigade is actually paying attention to the public support for the people of Ukraine they come up with the "Brilliant and humanitarian" decision to send refugee's to Rwanda with the favoured option that they stay there?

It just feels as if the UK government, no matter who they are, just wants to go back to the days of the Empire and alienate everybody by using assumed superior intellect. We are not in a cuddly world where everyone loves everyone, but we still need to stand up for what is right, for what matters. The bank balance of the worlds leaders is totally useless to the people they are supposed to represent.

- Forgive and Forget

Religious Sinner

As I reach for an answer to a question
I grasp for what I can see
The reason you give is a problem
Created for all history

A speculative thought causes anger
The direction of emotional rage
The hand that holds your freedom
As you lay naked in your cage

The dirt and blood are mixed
Like paint upon your breast
No more worries of everyday
You are the hang-mans guest.

Yet I still reach to touch you
To have you tell me more
About the God that brought you here
And made you a judgmental bore.

I need but I don't like you
I tried so hard to be your friend
And now because you worship it
Your God has brought your end

Do not think of yesterday
As though it was your last
Prepare yourself for battle
From religion you must fast

You said too much, you carried on
Even with a knife at your throat
And now because you preached out loud
You have become the sacrificial goat.

I reach for you, please don't cry
If you must you can say a prayer
Just remember it's because of faith
That the Hang-man has you there.

As you drop your neck will break
And so will my aching heart
For by bringing your God unto this world
You have ripped my world apart.

Surely there is another way in life for us all to co-exist, why do we need different Gods? There is an estimated 4200 different religions in the world today. Which one to worship surely should be down to the individual. All of the religions do however have one thing in common, the want for peace, the need for acceptance and the ability to forgive one's enemies.

However, there has been an estimated 10,000 distinct religions worldwide. About 84% of the world's population is affiliated with Christianity, Islam, Hinduism, Buddhism, or some form of folk religion. The religiously unaffiliated demographic includes those who do not identify with any particular religion, atheists, and agnostics.

So, what then is a religion?

The actual meaning of the word religion is simply a 'social gathering' and a belief in or the following of something which connects the gathering attendee's together. To be part of the religion you would have certain behaviours to follow, prayers to recite and many rituals and services that needed following with both passion and blood soaked commitment.

Earlier I mentioned the Dead Sea Scrolls, they were written approximately 300 years BC and finished roughly 100 years after the birth of the man known as "Jesus of Nazareth". No matter the religion you are following you would all have some sort of figure-head or prophet in which all of your vision and devotion would be centred. The one over-riding element in all religions is the different ways they are studied. Theology, Philosophy and Comparative Religion.

That then is the scientific explanation of what a religion is. The ethical description is open to your own judgement but overall it is the belief in an entity or a group of entities, and the following of rules laid down by the leaders of that faith. All I know and I admit in my opinion, religion is simply a way for a large institution to make a huge amount of money, by followers of that religion to murder others whose beliefs do not match their own. The churches I have been in have been nothing more than fashion shows and the best hat parade that constantly require compliments and one over the person sat in the pew next door. There are so many wrong parts of following a God which for me out weigh the positives tenfold.

One of the things I have always had conflict with is the Christian ability to forgive. The bible tells you that no matter what another person does to you, you must offer forgiveness and forget everything that has gone before.
But I can't help thinking where is the line drawn? Is there a limit to which a Christian work's? Once he or she has been wronged three times they cannot forgive again? I agree holding on to the pain someone else has caused you for too long can be destructive. Surely that is just human emotion and common sense?
So with this in mind, do we forgive those who bomb our cities? Do we say "Hey, it's OK, I forgive you?" I just can't get my head around it.

The Christian, and I say Christian just for explanation I know that there are many and varied religious teachings and followers, the religious follower then, their ability to just accept atrocities and put it down to the Devil and just carry on baffles me. As a true believer in God, whatever your calling may be, you are taught to accept everyone, well that doesn't happen for one. You are encouraged to help everyone, treat everyone as equals, to be tolerant and caring. To preserve and worship life. The question I ask again as before is why then most wars and atrocities in world that have been born out of a religious leader's belief in his own rules and not necessarily the rules listed by his specific religion.

There is a religious group called Jainism. They have been around for centuries and are in my opinion one of the reasons I find religion so confusing.

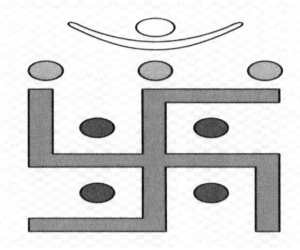

Jainism or Jain Dharma?

Jainism is a religion of non-violence. Non-destruction and equality to every living thing. It dates back to around a recorded date of c500 B.C., however it is thought to be much older than that.

This is what I find confusing.

Religion to me, what I have been taught and what I perceive to be is all about existing, living and growing, both physically and spiritually.
Jainists believe nothing should be killed to serve us. This includes any animal, bird, beast, fish or fowl. No plant should be picked to feed us, no vegetables, no fruit, no wheat to make bread. Nothing should ever die for us to live.
So what do Jainists eat?
Heavy duty followers have even been known to commit spiritual suicide by refusing to eat anything that has lived. Where is the religious sense in that?
One of their flags even has a Swastika displayed upon it.

We all know that the Swastika was used by Hitler's Nazi party during the war but it actually was the symbol for a cross used by the Roman Empire some two thousand years before, yet here we see the emblem used as part of a religious order

What I am trying to say here is that religion contradicts itself all of the time.

Going back to Forgiveness for a second.

As a Christian would you forgive someone like Hitler for his war crimes? As a Christian where you are encouraged to forgive could you forgive Hitler and his Nazi soldiers for murdering so many people? Where do you draw the line?
I know I am being dramatic and argumentative, but I am trying to understand.
Growing up in the 1970's every evening before bed we sat as a family to watch the news on TV. There was no SKY or Virgin then it was BBC or ITV or nothing. Living in Swansea every other program was in Welsh so the choice was cut even further. The usual reporters appeared before us to tell us of a Government bore calling another Government bore names, or how a film star had died or how the weather was going yet again to be terrible. Frequently however we were also told of the Troubles as they were called in Northern Ireland and how in the Middle East yet another British Missionary had been kidnapped by one of the many religious factions that were running rife.
One such man was Terry Waite, looking at this man who, with his big eyes, very tall stature and big bushy beard, he was bound to stand out in any crowd.
Waite was the Assistant for Anglican Communion Affairs for the then Archbishop of Canterbury, Robert Runcie, in the 1980s. As an envoy for the Church of England, he travelled to Lebanon to try to secure the release of four hostages, including the journalist John McCarthy. He was himself kidnapped and held captive from 1987 to 1991. Very often on the news a reporter would stand in front of Westminster Abbey for effect and tell us all how an envoy had been sent to attempt to free the British hostages being held. Very soon the ongoing saga of Waite's imprisonment would be mentioned almost every night. He spent a total of 1763 days in captivity with approximately 1460 in solitary confinement.
Terry Waite had successfully talked his way through many hostage release scenarios but his ongoing friendship with American Colonel Oliver North and his use of American Military transport made the group I.J.O. Islamic Jihad Organization see Waite as a valuable asset and bargaining tool. So on the news night after night we would be shown old footage of this larger than life man standing alongside Robert Runcie the then Archbishop of Canterbury dwarfing him in comparison.
Years later in 1997 I think, Terry Waite was speaking about his experiences at several meetings around the religious groups of Swansea University. After one such meeting he came for dinner with friends to the Restaurant I worked in at the time. After everyone had left and for all intense purposes we had finished work we sat for a short while talking to Waite. I was shocked to see this man who obviously with his great height and become a slight reflection physically of the man I used to see on TV. He told us all about his experiences at the hands of the I.J.O. and how he felt towards the men who individually hurt him so much.

So once again as with Harralan Popov a man who has given his life to his belief in goodness, in doing what is right and his God, is treated so badly.

From all religions and walks of life there has always been the need to publicly show your strength and non-wavering commitment to whatever God you believe in. During my life time I can recall many news reports and hearsay stories of people being executed for just not following a religion.
Then as we came into the age of the internet and global news, all of sudden we began to get graphic videos emerging on the world wide web showing missionaries, aid workers or military personnel publicly flogged, paraded and at its worst filmed having their heads cut off.

Two high profile examples of this were Alan Jenning and David Haines.

* Alan Henning (15 August 1967 – c. 3 October 2014) was an English taxicab driver-turned-volunteer humanitarian aid worker. He was the fourth Western hostage killed by Islamic State of Iraq and the Levant (ISIL) whose killing was publicised in a beheading video. Henning was captured during ISIL's occupation of the Syrian city of Al-Darna.

* David Cawthorne Haines (9 May 1970 – c. 13 September 2014) was a British aid worker who was captured by the Islamic State of Iraq and the Levant (ISIL) in early 2013 and beheaded in early September 2014.

Isil were so proud to show the world how barbaric they could be. How strong and powerful they were. Yet all they had actually done is capture two men who were there to do good, honest and humanitarian work. These men were not professional soldiers, they were not men who could fight their way out of trouble with skills learnt after years in the military, they were honest hard working men who just wanted to do some good in the world.

So what did they in fact achieve? Apart from decimating two families home here in the U.K.

Absolutely nothing.

Why did they do it?

They did to show strength, to tell the world that the God they believe in, their religion, their law is the true law, true God and only worthy religion.

The world is full of people who have done wrong at all levels who due to the forgiveness of Holy men and righteous snobs are now highly respectful in roles befitting only the highest in society.

The question I ask here as before is where is the line drawn in the sand? Who do we forgive, what crime is acceptable to be forgiven?

There is such horror in the world. Whenever I walk past the local Catholic Church I look around to see if the preacher is close by. I don't know why I wouldn't I think actually speak to him. However when I have walked past at church chucking out time I have heard him say "Go with the grace of God" or "May God protect you"

In the Bible it is claimed Jesus once said "Suffer the children and bring them to me"

It is suggested that Jesus as a preacher was quite ready and willing to sit with a group of children and discuss religion to them via stories he told. Whenever there is any sort of service going on the blessing of a child is always at the fore front of a service, or when there is a problem, a disaster we always look to take care of our future, our children first, and rightly so.

So if God is real how can he possibly let the terrible things that happen to children on a daily basis actually happen?

Just look at this list:

1/   Colombian serial killer Luis Garavito killed at least 138 young boys over his murderous history.

2/   Daniel Camargo Barbosa was a Colombian serial killer. It is believed that he raped and killed over 150 young girls in Colombia and Ecuador during the 1970s and 1980s.

3/   Over a period of 7 years, Ramadan Abdel Rehim Mansour raped and murdered at least 32 children.

4/   In 1981-1986, Robert Black kidnapped and murdered 4 young girls, aged 5-11.

5/   Nurse Beverly Allitt killed four children and tried to kill many more while working in a hospital in 1991.

6/   Ian Brady, along with his partner Myra Hindley, killed 5 children, aged 10-17, between 1963 and 1965.

7/   Dean Corll took the lives of at least 28 young boys over the course of 3 years starting in 1970. He was better known as the Candy Man since his family owned a candy factory in Texas

8/ Former clergyman Andras Pandy killed two of his wives and four children, along with the help of his daughter Agnes with whom he had a sexual   relationship. He was sentenced to life in prison in 1997.

9/ Fred West was an English serial killer who committed at least 12 murders between 1967 and 1987 in Gloucestershire, the majority with his second wife, Rosemary West. All the victims were young women, several his own children.

10/ The Soham murders occurred in Soham, Cambridgeshire, England, on 4 August 2002. The victims were two 10-year-old girls, Holly Marie Wells and Jessica Aimee Chapman. They were murdered by their school caretaker, Ian Huntley.

Just ten examples, but where was God to stop all of these horrific crimes from happening?

Nowhere, he, it, she whatever does not exist!

Just look at the Preachers accused of child sex abuse.

        If God was real in any guise at all would that entity allow such atrocities?
There have been quite literally thousands of priests accused of sexual abuse of a minor throughout the world. The children involved are mainly aged between 11years and 14 years old. The part of the world you live in doesn't help as these abusive attacks have happened all over the world.
These men, and they are all men, are the messengers of God. God's link to mankind and the purveyors of his word. If anybody was ever going to trust someone it would be a preacher you would trust.
Taking advantage of their position both in the church and the community, taking the trust of all of these young innocent people and grooming them to such an extent they don't know what is right, wrong or indifferent.
Yet when you look at the detail how many have actually been prosecuted? How many have had their identity and reputations saved by a church that will turn an eye to save face?
When the abuser is a movie star or TV star, and rightly so, they are named, shamed and prosecuted to the full extent of the law.
It's all about trust, it's all about face value and of course it's about money.
If we can't believe in their word, if we can't trust them to look after our children and if we can't trust in the law then we have nothing left to believe in, do we?

        My mother was the sort of person who, even though she enjoyed nothing more than a good gossip, she believed in giving everyone a chance, in being fair and to give that all important second chance. Unfortunately she was also someone who was hurt very easily and let down by so many people on so many occasions.
Through all of this she kept her faith and believed that no matter what God would help her get through every and any situation.

However God let the world down time and time again

Every time you see something horrific happening in the world unless it is a natural disaster or a political war you know it is going to have started because of religion. You know that there is a God of some sort driving this horror to happen.
There are still people being persecuted in certain countries for being black or for being gay or for believing in something or someone other than the masses.
So again I ask the question as I asked at the beginning "Do we need God ?"
We would all be equal, we would all be living as humans and not as brain washed beings.
The God in the Bible is a God of love and forgiveness. A God of wisdom and understanding. If this entity is real, and yes another question, wouldn't he, it accept any and every other denomination. wouldn't the blindly led follower accept all other faith's?
Yet Isis murders non believers, the Roman Catholic Church treats people like possession's and the wealth and pomp of the religious world makes a mockery of the worshippers who are hungry, cold and homeless.

All of these horrific acts–do we forgive those carrying them out?

Diary 3

Sitting here I wonder how or if it is possible for the so called leaders of our country can get any lower, stranger or indeed, stupid?

When we are being told that Russia are sending in trained assassins to wipe out the Ukrainian hierarchy, when yet again we see images of missiles hitting buildings and dead bodies laying unclaimed in the streets, and when back here in the UK almost everyday there is a news story of another murder, another rape and another report of child abuse and how the under resourced Police as brilliant as they are just haven't got the man power to deal with everything , we learn a Conservative party member, the same sect, sorry party as the Boris Brigade is watching pornography in the House of Commons.

Who are these people?

We live in a time when non-binary identification is possible and welcomed, we live in a time when same sex people can marry, we live in time that insists we treat people fairly at all times. Not it seems if you are a member of the Conservative party. Saying that I don't really think it helps that a Labour party member was asked on the radio today about her thoughts on the porn star film buff she responds that the whole set up of Westminster is wrong and built for men because………wait for it………

"There is only one ironing board"

Now I admit I am just a little bit bonkers, but I would like to think I know what is right or wrong. Our political leaders are just wrong, wrong in every way.

Ethics = none

Common Sense = don't make me laugh

Decency = Not a chance

Honesty? You decide!

- The Man himself?

As I briefly mentioned earlier I am fully aware and acknowledge the fact that Jesus indeed did live and was a preacher of sorts. As we have already heard the 'Dead Sea Scrolls' did mention Jesus and the Twelve Apostles but never does it suggest a holy or unearthly presence in Jesus. We are also taught at Sunday school that the Bible books of Mathew, Mark, Luke and John are the true written accounts of Jesus. However, if you actually read these books of the bible, a mention of the Messiah is very hard to find.

At the time of the Roman Emperor Nero and his infamous fiddling whilst Rome burnt, the faction know as Christians were blamed for starting the fire, of course we know Nero started the fire himself just to blame the Christians. We are fully aware that the group that followed the man called 'Jesus' had claimed he was the Christ and every film and book we are shown about him suggests a man of peace and love. Indeed the Dead Sea Scrolls agree with this, never however is it claimed that the Twelve Apostles were peaceful, on the contrary, they were known as what I suppose today we would call terrorists.

Religion, or *Religio,* never really existed as a 'thing' until the 16th or 17th century, yes Christianity, Buddhism and most of the Islamic faiths have been around for much longer but a faith was only called a Religion recently. You simply followed and believed and you lived your life to those rules for example. Another example of this was the fact that to be Jewish and to follow Judaism was a matter of Race, not a religion. It is only when the world was starting to become 'Westernised' that the way you lived was seen as being different from the way you worshipped, one had nothing to do with the other. There are millions of people in the world who call Jesus the Son of God, there are just as many sceptics who call him a myth and legend.

Living at this time for anyone was difficult. You would spend most of your day searching for food for the family evening meal. There would be prayer rituals throughout the day and of course if you had a trade, fisherman, carpenter or even a tax collector, you of course had your job to do. Whether you believe the bible stories or the Dead Sea Scrolls you have to accept the man Jesus would have had to work, take on his 'fathers' trade to make money. If the Scrolls are to be believed Jesus was a fisherman with his father working out of their village, Qumran. As was typical of the day by the age of 12 years old he would have been married and his whole life would be based on the daily welfare of his family.

We know he preached, we know he joined the Twelve Apostles but other than these two facts, what is said in the Dead Sea Scrolls and what is claimed by the gospels couldn't be any further apart. The 'Monastery of Flagellation' is a 700 year old institute in the area of historic Jerusalem that deals with, and welcomes, archaeological investigations into the bible and its characters. The Franciscan Mission is laboured with looking after the historic site's in the area and, since the 19th century, to excavate them according to scientific principles. Father Alliata who is leading the archaeology welcomes visitors with a sceptical eye saying, "Whether or not Jesus did exist cannot be proved, or disproved by archaeology, i.e. a specific person, after 2000 years."

The Gospel's according to Matthew, Mark, Luke and John were written in the latter part of the first century and unfortunately for the world of religion there is very little archaeological evidence that supports the stories of the Gospel. As Father Aliata said "There is no historical find that can or cannot prove the man, Jesus Christ, lived" However there are finds we can touch, we can see that prove certain things were real. For example there is a cave with images of John the Baptist painted on the walls, were there is a shallow well where people would immerse their bodies to 'wash away all evil', there is even a small right foot shaped hole in the ground where people would insert their right foot to be washed as part of the ritual. We know many of the actions mentioned generally 'did' happen, crucifixion, the Passover, the census to give three examples. Yet there is no 'diary' giving dates, times and facts about the people of the day. The only 'fact' the four gospels agree upon is the amount of time which passed between Jesus' entry into Jerusalem and the time that Jesus was arrested in the garden of Gethsemane, this is also written in the Dead Sea Scrolls.

- Undoing Innocence

In the past thirty years, thirty-seven Roman Catholic dioceses have filed for bankruptcy. Why is this? Maybe due to the financial problems the whole world appears to be facing right now is having an effect on our disposable income? The average size of a typical congregation has fallen by more than 40% in the same period of time in churches all over the world. The number of priests who are on a 'period of reflection' or having an amount of time to consolidate their faith has grown, as has the number of Holy leaders who, especially if they were in office in the 1980's, have suddenly been moved to locations many, many churches away from there desired locations. Why?

There is a group of religious leaders who just like most other people in the world believe there is a current and historical problem in the church. 'Bishop Accountability', is an organization that tracks accusations, lists more than 6,400 priests or other Catholic Church personnel who have been accused of sexual abuse since the release of a breakthrough study, no database tracks how many priests have been prosecuted for child abuse. In the past thirty years or so there have been a reported 210,000 cases of child sexual abuse by a priest or other member of the church.

Just a couple of examples:

Germany

In June, Pope Francis rejected an offer by top German bishop Reinhard Marx to resign over the Church's "institutional and systemic failure" in handling child sexual abuse in the western city of Cologne. It revealed that 314 minors, mostly boys under the age of 14, were sexually abused there between 1975 and 2018. A German Bishops' Conference study in 2018 had previously revealed widespread sexual abuse by German clergy.

It found that 1,670 clergymen had committed some type of sexual attack against 3,677 minors, mostly boys under 13, between 1946 and 2014, while saying this was almost certainly an underestimate.

Most perpetrators have not been punished and the church grants compensation on a case-by-case basis, without transparency.

United States

In 2002, the Boston Globe revealed the massive scale of sexual abuse on children in the Boston diocese and efforts by the Catholic hierarchy to cover it up.

In 2004, a church commission published a report requiring clergy to report suspicions of sexual assault. According to lawyers, more than 11,000 complaints have been lodged in the US by victims of priests. Dioceses have paid out hundreds of millions of dollars in out of court settlements. Victims associations say that these pay-outs allow the church to escape justice.

A grand jury investigation into Pennsylvania dioceses in 2018 exposed the systematic cover-up by the church of abuse by "over 300 predator priests". More than 1,000 child victims were cited. Cardinal Donald Wuerl, accused of a cover-up, resigned. In 2019, Pope Francis defrocked former American cardinal Theodore McCarrick in a first for the church.

Several dioceses have since opened their archives, revealing that hundreds of priests had been suspected of abusing minors.

Don't think for one moment the United Kingdom escapes. Church run orphanages were in practically every major town and city from the whole of Ireland, the most Northern points of Scotland, the deepest valleys of Wales and of course the industrial hearts such as London and Birmingham. If you break down the total number of accusations of sex abuse against children since 1930 when they started to be recorded, (so who knows how many the church were guilty of before), it would average 15,000 accusations a year. Thats 1,380,000 possible cases that the church have been fully aware, have moved the accused before anything formal has happened against them or simply it has been swept under the carpet. There is not however a record of actual convictions.

In line with the current climate against such behaviours the Catholic Church has had to finally take notice
.

The Vatican recently announced the defrocking of 848 priests who had admitted raping or molesting children a further 2,572 have taken lesser sanctions. The United Nations has since come out and made sexual abuse against children a formal form of torture. The opinion amongst legal experts around the world claim this could, making sexual abuse a torture, open the doors for many, many more accusations and more importantly, prosecutions.
That is the official look at what is going on. However, if you look at just these numbers from just the few examples above just imagine how horrifically high the actual number must be? How many events went un-reported?

After several highly reported cases hit the headlines concerning TV celebrities, pop stars and so on, the visibility of child sexual abuse was at last hitting the media for the world to see. It didn't matter it appears, how high up the religious ladder you were for there to be some sort of involvement.

The former Archbishop of Westminster, Cardinal Cormac Murphy O'Connor was reportedly aware of allegations against Father Michael Hill and still let him take up position in Gatwick Airport as the chaplain. Hill went on then to abuse again. He was jailed after pleading guilty to nine separate accounts of abuse. Cardinal Murphy O'Connor went on to say he regretted deeply what had happened but, he was acting on advise from behavioural specialists.

No matter what religious body you belong to, a part of or lead you have a responsibility to the congregations you are meant to serve, are you not? In other words how many of the possible 1,380,000 abuse accusations by members of the clergy have been prosecuted or even investigated?

Over the last few months more evidence has emerged of systematic child abuse within the Catholic church from around the world.

Here in Wales and England there are a new 37 cases of priests who have committed sexual crimes against children It contains details of convictions for sexual abuse and the sentences handed down. As many of the cases are said to be historic the number of cases dropped due to the ill health of priests involved or the fact that they may have already died can never be known.

After Judge Lord Nolan together with Cardinal Murphy O'Connor carried out a full report on Child Protection, and later on after Lord Nolan and indeed the Pope made public apologies in failings on behalf of the church to protect children, the Catholic authorities in England and Wales created a body called the Church Office for Protection of Children and Vulnerable Adults (COPCA) headed by the now Archbishop of Westminster Vince Nichols. The latest in a very long catalogue of abuse stories has been the revelation that 216,000 children have been sexually abused by the clergy in France since 1950. That works out at 8.22 cases every day. So roughly 8/9 kids every day in France since 1950 have had their lives ruined. I couldn't find the answer online anywhere but, I wonder just how many have gone on to take their own lives?

When Pope Francis found out he gave out a statement giving his 'profound sadness and pain' but hoped for redemption. On the back of this the Vatican ordered an investigation into paedophilia within the church, something that was totally unprecedented by any Vicar of Christ. Due to the knowledge gained it was made very public that the Vatican would not accept such abuse and in fact the Vatican's own 'In house laws' now made it a criminal offence. Now, why not always!!?

However, the church is still dogged by massive sexual abuse cover up's right up to the very top of the holy tree.

The history of sexual abuse by priests as far back as records began, however only ever being brought to any sort of justice in the 1950's. It wasn't until 4000+ cases hit the headlines in both the USA and Canada in the 1980's was there global visibility of the problem. At the start of the 2000's stories started to emerge from Ireland, the UK and Australia, from Argentina, Austria and Rome itself. By the mid 2000's and even though the fact that child sexual abuse was everywhere in the world, and still being carried out by priests, it wasn't until the movie "Spotlight" in 2015 that the whole background of the issue, was made known to us. How priests were not getting sanctioned or more importantly arrested because when the abuse came to light the priest was simply moved to a far off parish by the church hierarchy.

In 2017 a number of investigations around the world began, in Australia it was found that child sexual abuse was not only in churches. It was happening in schools, youth clubs and day centres. However, all of these facilities were being run by priests.

In Ireland there were claims of thousands of abuse victims coming forward that were brought up in orphanages, all run by the church. In France the head of the investigation said that even though it would be nice to think the abuse had been stopped it is still going on somewhere and people need to come forward. He added that proven historic cases should be able to open the gates for some sort of compensation for its victims. Yet still it goes on. Still more and more historic cases are coming to light and more and more high ranking clergy members are being investigated.

These people are the men and women that as kids we are taught to respect, taught to be in awe of and as kids in the 1970's Welsh valleys, the fire breathing Vicars we had, we were taught to fear them. I can remember as a youngster going to Tabernacle Welsh Baptist Church in Swansea with my mother. I must of been 4 maybe 5 years old. The Pastor was Reverend W.J. A tall true Welshman with white hair and piercing soul-less eyes. He was terrifying.

Everything mentioned here is on national record, but why? Not why are we told about these facts, the question is why are we so shocked when it is talked about? This evidence shows that child abuse by the church, from every faith I would hazard a guess, child abuse has been happening for years and years. The whole idea of the church is about the good things we can do for each other, about love and peace and forgiveness. Yet practically every news story concerning the church, of whatever faith, is a negative one. When a priest has been involved in child sex abuse how can they go into the confession with a parishioner with any sort of decency? Knowing the behaviours they may have been involved in how can they meet, greet and befriend the parents without showing any guilt or apparent remorse?

Diary 4

Today is the 10th day of my second dose of Covid-19. This episode has not been as bad as the last, I'm guessing because the weather is so different. My first bout was in the middle of winter and now we are in the middle of a heatwave. I have been into work for 4 days in between but yesterday I just couldn't breathe properly. Luckily I am testing negative now so i will try to go to work again tomorrow.

Just like so many others the past couple of years have been terrible, for all sorts of reasons and of course reasons of varying importance. Again just like so many others finances have completely collapsed for Jo and I, but we are trying hard to build and I am sure we will do it.

- Excuses, the weapons and why?

The whole world has so much to put up with. Just a few examples:

    1 The Russian invasion of the Ukraine
    2 The ever present threat of the Covid 19 plague
    3 The horrendous future we all face financially in the current climate
    4 The constant battle to feed our family, heat our homes and just live

All over the world over the past two years or more, as like generations past, people have gone to church, knelt and prayed for help in these most tumultuous of times. There have been cries for help and prayers for forgiveness. There are food banks and crisis loans and people all over the world are on their knee's just looking for that extra bit of love.

On September 8th this year, 2022, here in the United Kingdom Her Majesty Queen Elizabeth II passed away. She had been our Monarch for 71 years and reached the fruitful age of 96 years old. I saw her only once in person back in 1977 when she opened the new Leisure Centre in Swansea during her Silver Jubilee year. As head of the Church of England the day of her funeral had all of the religious and Royal pomp you would expect. For four days leading up to the funeral the coffin of our lady sat in Westminster hall whilst members of the public walked past after standing in line for up to 30 hours, then spent just 30 seconds with bowed head and a tear to pay respects. There were services at Westminster Abbey and later at Windsor Castle all of which were televised for the world to see. I agree with the respect the Queen as a person and as our Monarch received, I agree with the ceremony played out by her family and other heads of state. I am very proud of the new era in the Royal family and I must say King Charles III has been a true and worthy Monarch since the death of his mother. I wish him a long and peaceful reign.

There is so much money on show however in all religious services you just have to ask yourself would even half of the wealth on display be better served feeding the many poor and homeless followers that God still demands.

'Bellum Sacrum' is Latin for a battle or War that is started purely to defend, or impose, a religious following. Where there is a 'Holy War', such as the conflict still going on in parts of the Middle East (Israel, Palestine for example) are very often discounted as such purely due to the financial implications, both positive and negative that such a war creates.

Scholars of the world believe there is almost always another reason for such a conflict to be started. For example; the current war in Ukraine according to Putin, Russia's leader, that Ukraine is part of Russia historically therefore should once again live under the hammer and sickle. The truth is nothing however to do with history it is purely financial and power that drives the death we see everyday on the news. Not religion I know, but the idea is the same. It is nothing to do with history but everything to do with power.

Of course it depends on your own interpretation of religion as to whether a war is or is not influenced as such. There have been 1763 'Legal' wars in recorded history with only 121 recorded as a religious war (6.87%), however 100 of those 121 have been named as the deadliest wars ever fought. A religious war usually is reported as having no real battles, more one side wiping out another because of the God, they do or don't follow. An example would be the Spanish extermination of the Inca/Aztec people in the 16th century.

At the time of writing this passage I can see people dressing the outside of their houses and hanging lanterns and plastic pumpkins around their gardens ready for next weeks, American led, Halloween festival. All Hallows Eve never had any sort of root or history that had anything to do with evil. On the contrary, All Hallows Eve was the day before 'All Saints' are honoured. Throughout history 'Saints' have been a part of our religious history, but the dressing up as ghosts and monsters on October 31st is most definitely an American creation as a party.

In the time of the bible stories All Hallows Eve was considered the best day to get married, to have a birthday or to celebrate something good, or to even die. For it was the only day the intervention and help of the devil was acceptable. Halloween is a night of great evil. But really, it's a night of great evil only because the devil is invoked in some of the customs and some of the practices. If it were nothing but a harvest festival, it probably wouldn't amount to much. The question is: Is there really a devil, and are there demons in a spirit world that come out on Halloween or at other times? So to celebrate the Saints honoured by religion you are encouraged to welcome the devil into your home. Very soon we will celebrate Christmas, which of course is said to represent the birth of Jesus Christ. Once again Religion and money go hand in hand. It was only during and after the Protestant Reformation in the 17th century, that individuals started following and promoting a particular religious view. At the same time exploration of the world was booming and so people were coming into contact with new Gods, and of course, Gods were forced onto indigenous people from around the world. Books such as the Bible, the Quran and indeed all other texts reporting the acts of a prophet had no concept of a religion because it was assumed if you are reading the texts, then that is the way you live your life. It is not a choice to follow, it is your duty. In the Quran for example, the Arabic word din is often translated as "religion" in modern translations, but up to the mid-17th century, translators expressed din as "law". So putting it simply, what we call Religion today, before the 17th century was the law by which you were expected to live your life.

In 2015 a review was carried out looking at the subject of violence within religious matters, it could not disprove the fact that violence and religion around the world went hand in hand.

As I stated in an earlier chapter my mother was brought up as a Welsh Baptist. The older my mother got the more devout she became. At the same time my brother was a serving soldier in the British Army stationed in Northern Ireland. The conflict we know as "The Troubles", but what exactly was the trouble? Growing up I was always led to b was the Protestant Faith against the people who followed the Roman Catholic Faith. In reality it was two separate sectarian groups who wanted the power.

The Fertile Crescent is better known as the Middle East. The area covers everything from Egypt to Turkey, from Cyprus to Iran & Iraq and everything surrounding and in between. It is home to what is called the "Holly Land", it is also home to some of the most brutal and continuous wars in history.

(By the way; a battle can only be called a 'war' if there are at least 100 deaths because of it).

All of the above are a taste of the effect and affect religion has had on the world.

To look at just one 'religious war' in detail let's look at probably the most powerful situation, one of the oldest and most deadly conflicts.

The Israeli–Palestinian conflict is one of the world's most enduring conflicts, beginning in the mid-20th century. Various attempts have been made to resolve the conflict as part of the Israeli–Palestinian peace process, alongside other efforts to resolve the broader Arab–Israeli conflict. The whole geography of the conflict is according to religious scholars, The Holy Land. Whether you believe the biblical account of Jesus being born in Bethlehem or the Dead Sea Scrolls claim he was born in Qumran, the common fact is that he was born in an area so consumed by war for so long. From the Romans who occupied the area for hundreds of years including the time of Jesus, to today where shells are still being dropped on a regular basis, namely around the Gaza strip.

The current Israeli-Palestinian status quo began following Israeli military occupation of the Palestinian territories in the 1967 Six-Day War.

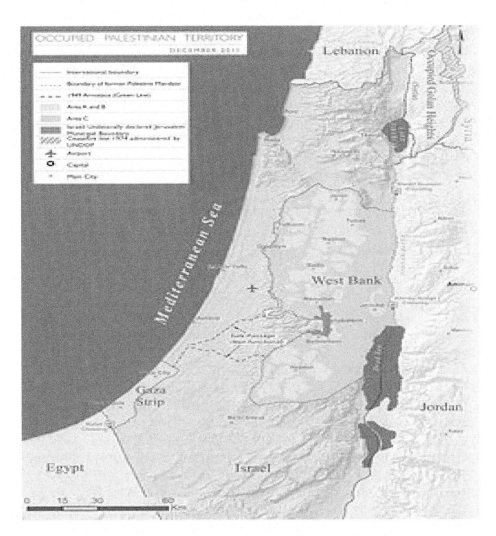

The Dead Sea, to the South East of the West Bank is the home of so many stories from the bible. Indeed, all of the area shown in this map are said to have been the home of the birth of Christianity. The Oslo Accord which was written between 1993 and 1995 got the two warring factions, the Israeli and Palestine forces, together and a compromise on land, boundaries and settlements was agreed. However opinion currently suggests the idea of living peacefully together appears to be fading very fast. There has been a constant threat of bombings, murders and all sorts of accusations going on but over the past couple of years the tensions seem to be escalating.

The one place on Earth where, if you believe in any of the Christian faiths, you would expect love, understanding, forgiveness and peace to exist, Israel and the Holy Land, remains one of the most deadly places to live. From the Jewish faith to the Roman Catholic Church, from Muslims, to the Baptist Christian Faith the whole world believes in something yet there still can't be peace.

One example of a mixture of faiths is the Island of Sri Lanka. During a recent census the total population was estimated at 23 million (midyear 2021). The 2012 national census, which provides the most recent available data, lists the population as 70.2 percent Buddhist, 12.6 percent Hindu, 9.7 percent Muslim, and 7.4 percent Christian. So many faiths in one nation but a nation which has been affected by conflict for many years. Surely the different faiths should live along side each other, isn't that the honourable and Holy thing to do?

Of course a classic example of all of this, are the 'Crusades'. The Knights Templar or Knights of Christ along with the likes of Richard the Lionheart and his armies who invaded the Middle East to take it back 'off' the Muslim faith which was now prominent in the area. One of the main goals being to take back control of Jerusalem. Legends abound with stories of treasure such as the Arc of the Covenant being captured at the time. All through the ages of man the need to push your faith and beliefs has been paramount. The need to kill, to destroy and control your population by threats of an afterlife of fire if they do not follow what you are telling them is the 'only' true God!

Take a look for yourself at everything in history that mentions a war or battle, the underlining reason almost every time is God!

Diary 5

This week in the United Kingdom, and indeed for the past 3 years, our political system and leaders have been in an utter and complete mess. The past 4 months has seen 3 different Prime Ministers in office, all part of the Conservative party.

The reason I put it in here is for me the reason why we fail in the UK today. The Rt Hon Rishi Sunak has been voted in as our new Prime Minister. I am not a Conservative supporter but I have to say Mr. Sunak talks with sense, factually and without spin. We need to give him a chance as a politician to make his mark.

However, on the news yesterday and on various "Call in" shows the only 2 things people could talk about were how much money his wife is worth and the fact that he is of Asian decent. There was hardly anything about his career in politics so far and the fact that even during the Covid pandemic when as Chancellor, Mr. Sunak said it as it was, "Financially times are going to be very difficult for a number of years" Why does his religious background or the colour of his skin matter?

- Is there a Difference?

There are an estimated 4200 different religions in the world today. The five major religions or philosophies—are atheism, Buddhism, Hinduism, Islam, and Christianity. Of course Christianity covers many religions such as the Jewish, Baptist and Roman Catholic faiths. Most people follow a particular faith due to their family heritage, ethnic up bringing or regional expectations

Christianity has its roots in Judaism. In the Bible the book of Deuteronomy 6:4—a verse of scripture within both Judaism and Christianity—states, "The Lord our God, the Lord is One." Which one? It is readily agreed that the Jesus mentioned in both the Bible and the Dead Sea Scrolls is the same Jesus followed in the Muslim faith, but is the God followed the same one? According to the Christian word God is in fact the 'Holy Trinity', so he /she is God and Jesus and the Holy Spirit.

(notice my political correct comment?)

The author C. S. Lewis, said the three dimensions of space—length, width, and height—which all exist in the same space, yet are distinctly different illustrate this mystery more clearly. Looking at this then, God created man in his own image. Omnipotent power creates a world in six days, rests on the seventh. God designs a species to look and be just as he is. Yet, all of Gods power cannot keep this species as he would want. Apart from the devil, the apple and the garden, why can't God stop Cancer's or other deadly conditions? Would a God of love really bestow such horrific ailments onto his creation? Nobody can either prove or disprove a God or God's do or don't exist, Christianity in particular reaches into the hearts of its followers, the supernatural element of believing in God is all about how it, he/she makes you feel.

The Welsh Baptist faith was everything to my mother– a faith, a calling, a belief and for a long time an obsession. Ethel Pauline Ellis was born into a household full of love and religion from her mother and hate, alcohol and violence from her father. Growing up and indeed when after divorcing my father religion wasn't as important as going to church on a Sunday for appearance and family brownie points. She was trying so hard to achieve acceptance from her sister Sonia, the nearest in age and geography but still lightyears away apart. Over the years going to church became a ritual we as kids were dragged into and very soon it went from Sunday evening to Sunday morning, afternoon and evening and then apart from Sunday there was Monday and Wednesday evenings, Thursday morning and Friday afternoon. Very soon after she took on the role as church cleaner so the church became a seven day's a week habit. The whole 'going to church' thing became far more than listening to her God's stories, everything centred around church. Everything my mother did was to do with the church in one way or another yet on so many ways before and after my mothers death the church let her down. When sat in her living room at home my mother was never too far away from a notebook and pen which ultimately sat next to one of her many copies of the Bible.

Whilst watching TV or just sitting to relax she would be writing verses and prayers of her own design. Everything she wrote in one way or another was thanking

God or explaining to whoever was to read the work, exactly who God is and how he/she can make your life better. Seeing my mother slowly killing herself with her cigarettes and very little food, with her heavy breathing and constant coughing and the deepest sadness which I saw in her eyes every time I looked at her, as long as she had her God by her side as she believed she was happy.

My mother died on May 2nd 2005 which that year was the Bank Holiday Monday. Due to the Bank Holiday and due to a heavy bought of flu around at that time the number of deaths in the area was much higher than usual for the time of year. This meant there was almost a 3 week delay for the funeral to take place. There was however, still a huge amount of organising that had to be done. Her Council house had to be emptied, for which the Council gave us until the end of the week or they were going to charge another weeks rent. All of a sudden the religious groupies that spent hours around her bed praying were nowhere to be seen. Again I state these Christian men and women who my mother called her family, her brothers and sisters under God, yet they still asked me to PAY to hold her funeral service in the church she had given so much to.

There is also the Gnostic Bible which gives similar stories to the standard bible washed down with a totally different view than the scriptures and what they say suggest. It is here we learn Jesus was married to Mary Magdalene, we also learn he survived the cross, just as the Dead Sea Scrolls suggest. Then again, how would anyone really know if hr or anyone was alive coming off the cross. In reality the family and crowds of gawpers were kept quite a distance from the crucifixions and not up close and personal as portrayed in film, book and legend.

- The Jerusalem Puzzle

One of the most important prophets of the bible is the legend, Moses. The Jewish child brought up by an Egyptian princess, found in a basket floating on the Nile having been placed there in an attempt to hide him from the Pharoah's soldiers who had been ordered to kill all new born Jewish boys, placed there by his mother. We all know the stories that follow up until the point Moses is supposed to have died age 120 years old on Mount Nebo, in full view of the 'Promised Land'.

The trouble is that not any two historical experts can agree his date of birth, age at death or any of the stories in between. In reality, can it be assumed that Moses never actually lived? It is obvious to me that whilst trying to build a legend to include in the Bible someone has created this figure to try and show the miracle's that were supposed to have happened in the hope to gain belief. We have mentioned in this work that there have been many descriptive stories about Jesus. We have the version known to most which is taken from the Bible. Plus we have the account of the man called Jesus, whose name in Hebrew was "Yeshua" which translates in English as Joshua, found in the Dead Sea Scrolls. Which Jesus you believe in is of course entirely up to you. The faith you follow or not, again is up to you. Yet if you are someone like me who struggles with just believing, I need proof, I need facts, I need stories that can be logically explained.

This week in Egypt a huge tomb has been found with approximately 200 mummies and what appears to be the sarcophagus of an Egyptian Queen. Could this be the much sought after tomb of the last ever Pharaoh and the most famous of Queens, Cleopatra? If it turns out to be the great Queens resting place or just another of the many other rulers we will know because of the great things that may or may not be found.

When a police force detects and solves a crime at whatever level they can get an answer to every question by the evidence that they can collect—the facts!

Every historical fact we know is due to the detail we find, written or physical. The evidence we do have regarding the church and religion comes from the Bible or equivalent and the Dead Sea Scrolls.

Constantine the Great, was Roman emperor from AD 306 to 337, and the first to convert to Christianity. Born in Naissus, Dacia Mediterranea (now Serbia), he was the son of Flavius Constantius, a Roman army officer of Illyrian origin who had been one of the four rulers of the Tetrarchy. His mother, Helena, was a Greek Christian. Constantine grew up as a pagan and in later life something of a catechumen. Catechumen was a form of following and teaching Christianity to people, mainly children, in a simple and uncomplicated way.

Before actually turning to Christianity, Constantine realised he needed somehow, to manage this new faction growing in strength. As he grew up with a mother who already followed the faith the more he looked into controlling it the more he began to believe in

Christianity. Apart from being a Roman Emperor who was turning to an outlawed faith, he was also a very intelligent tactician.

Constantine knew if he could build this man 'Jesus of Nazareth' into a legend he could also control the faith. However the more he listened to the word of Jesus the more he was drawn in.

Another of the great writers of the era was Flavius Josephus, c. 37 – c. 100 he was a first-century Romano-Jewish historian and military leader, best known for The Jewish War, who was born in Jerusalem—then part of Roman Judea—to a father of priestly descent and a mother who claimed royal ancestry. He initially fought against the Romans during the First Jewish–Roman War as head of Jewish forces in Galilee, until surrendering in 67 AD to Roman forces led by Vespasian after the six-week siege of Yodfat. Josephus claimed the Jewish Messianic prophecies that initiated the First Jewish–Roman War made reference to Vespasian becoming Emperor of Rome. In response, Vespasian decided to keep Josephus as a slave and presumably interpreter. After Vespasian became Emperor in 69 AD, he granted Josephus his freedom, at which time Josephus assumed the emperor's family name of Flavius.

Soon after he fully converted to the Roman way of life. He was granted Roman status and soon landed the role of advisor and translator to Titus during the battle for Jerusalem. There are many written stories that he knew the man Jesus, actually he would have only been born around the year of the crucifixion.

Every part of the story being told about Jesus from whichever author of the time, eventually led to the city of Jerusalem.

All of the parties at the time, whether it be Romans, Greeks or Israelites believed everything was centred around the city.

Jerusalem

There is a legend that Jerusalem is a mother who had three children. In chronological order, Judaism, Christianity and Islam. Unfortunately as with most siblings the rivalry became very painful to live through.

Situated in the Middle East it is one of the oldest named cities in the world. It is to be found in the area of Israel which as been claimed by many religions for eon's.

Both Israelis and Palestinians claim Jerusalem as their capital, as Israel maintains its primary governmental institutions there and the State of Palestine ultimately foresees it as its seat of power. Because of this dispute, neither claim is widely recognized internationally. The first record of a settlement being there date as far back as 4000BCE, this was to become the area called the "City of David".

Jerusalem has been destroyed twice, attacked 52 times, besieged at least 23 times and been occupied around 44 times.

Josephus had an audience made up specifically from Greek and Roman backgrounds and so when he wrote about both the war of Jerusalem and the Jewish race itself he was giving another side to stories that could often be found in the Bible.

The area was named as Urusalim in ancient Egyptian writings and so the name Jerusalem itself was adopted on this Canaanite settlement in about 1400BCE.

Modern Day Jerusalem photographed from Hebron

We know now the history of the area, how it was written about and how so many stories that are connected with the bible. Of course the main story concerns the arrival of Jesus into the city, of how he is betrayed by Judas and after several conversations with hierarchy he is put to death only to raise again.

Diary 6

Due much to the Russian invasion and continued attack on Ukraine, the whole of Europe is experiencing fuel shortages. Gas, Electricity and Oil are currently at a price that many of the suppliers have massively increased their charges. The Government have over the past two months, here in the UK, have put caps on the amount that the energy suppliers can charge us, but the amount is being changed by whatever millionaire politician is in charge of the country this week. The Autumn statement this week has told us that we are going to be at least another 3.7% worse off again in our pay packets. The oil Giant 'Shell' announced huge profits again and still prices go up.

- Betrayal of the Church

Chapter 3 of this book mentioned the help that the Roman Catholic church gave to the Nazi high ranking officers to escape the clutches of the ever advancing allies. This actioned due to the Pope at the time, Pope Pius XIII believing the Nazi war machine was not going to be as bad as any Communist army could have. The Vatican also believed it wouldn't be as bad as having the Nazi party in charge of Europe as it would being governed by Communists.

In short the whole religious essence of Europe at that time was completely messed up. Adolf Hitler contrary to belief wasn't German, he was from Austria which has always had a large Jewish community. Hitler gained popular support by attacking the Treaty of Versailles and promoting pan-Germanism, anti-Semitism and anti-communism with charismatic oratory and Nazi propaganda. He frequently denounced international capitalism and communism as part of a Jewish conspiracy. What he failed to recall however was the fact his early education, especially with his art, his teachers were all Jewish. Hitler and his band of Nazi warriors blamed the entire Jewish race for current state of German finances and for the negative way Germany came out of World War I. Such places as the concentration camps were already in place as prisons or holding camps for other reasons, political activists for example. The Nazi leadership started to send Jews from all parts of Europe that they hand hold over, to the camps. The rest is an horrific history of murder we are all to familiar with.

The Nokmim also referred to as The Avengers or the Jewish Avengers, were a Jewish partisan militia, formed by Abba Kovner and his lieutenants Vitka Kempner and RozkaKorczak from the surviving remnants of the United Partisan Organization (Fareynikte Partizaner Organizatsye), which operated in Lithuania under Soviet command. Kovner wanted to kill men, women and children, he didn't care if they were innocent of any crimes carried out by the army, and they were Germans. The group wanted to kill 6million Germans, the number of Jewish people killed by the Holocaust. Unfortunately for them when the ship they were travelling on was nearing Toulon in France the British Soldiers on board noticed their papers were forged. Before being caught they threw all of the poison overboard, so plan B kicked in. The plan was to poison the water supplies of major cities, Berlin, Nuremberg, and Munich.

On a smaller scale in a plan which was apparently agreed upon by the Israeli President Chaim Weissemen, was to poison 3000 loaves of bread with arsenic that was to be served to SS Officers that were being held after the war in Stalag 13, an American Prisoner of War Camp.

Out of the 4000 inmates at the camp some 2300 were affected with varying levels of sickness and about 400 SS soldiers actually dying, however this has been refuted with no actual proof of any deaths having been recorded.

This is just one example of how, and there are many, many such examples, of how one group of men, the Nazi leadership in this case, used the religion and / or race of a group of people to massacre them.

As a non Christian looking at the way a Christian is purported to live I can't help looking at the Ten Commandments with a certain amount of irony and humour. The Ten laws of God are made up of you can't do this or that, you shouldn't do this or have that, where is the freedom to choose.

An example; "Thou should worship no idol or any craven image", what then is a crucifix if it isn't an idol?

How many churches can you go into and see a massive crucifix hanging from the ceiling at the front, or a 5ft tall marble statue depicting what Mary looked like. There are paintings galore of Jesus and God. There are paintings of the Last Supper and paintings of a magical white beam of light showing us the way to heaven.

These are only examples but there are thousands, aren't these idol's that being worshipped? Aren't the paintings of Jesus that holy men kneel down in front of to prey, craven images?

You shall keep the Sabbath day holy. Which one?

We know in the Christian world that Sunday is the Sabbath because as per Gods creation in Exodus it is a day of rest. In Jewish religion it differs, according to halakha (Jewish religious law), Shabbat is observed from a few minutes before sunset on Friday evening until the appearance of three stars in the sky on Saturday night.

Even though many of the other stories and rules can be delved into with a tooth pick to bring out inconsistencies, the other to look at is;

Thou shalt not murder. Where do I start?

If you wanted to list the worst mass murderer's of all time who would you include?

Genghis Khan killed thousands, the Nazi's of Hitler's Germany killed an estimated 6 million Jews, even the gothic Count Dracula, the real Vlad Tsepesh, Vlad the Impaler is said to have killed hundreds of thousands of his enemies drinking their drained blood as he thought it would give him their power. The Imperial Japanese Army killed thousands as did various Zsars and leaders of the former USSR. All through history even up to the various warring factions still fighting throughout the world today people have died at the hand or command of another.

However even if you bunch all of these together, strip them down and take away all logical reasoning, the underlining fault is religion, a greed for power and wealth, a ruthless attraction to someone else's land.

Throughout the world and throughout millennia the Roman Catholic Church has been responsible for more deaths than any other body.

When Adolf Hitler became Chancellor of Germany in 1933 as mentioned above, it was decided that some sort of truce would have to be agreed with the Roman Catholic and the Nazi party. Luckily for the Nazi's Rome thought as Hitler was so against the Communist's of Russia he would be worth siding with.

So much so that the Pope formed a difficult if jointly enterprising relationship with Hitler.

There are indeed many photographs of Roman Catholic Cardinals saluting the Swastika. One of the holy fathers even being heard as he prayed:

" We give thanks to our Lord my God and Adolf Hitler "

This is fact not a made up statement.

Once again I am thrown into a tumble dryer of confusion and fact, of hearsay and rumour.

The holiest embodiment (their opinion) of the word of God, the Roman Catholic Church was in league with the most hated and evil group of leaders the world has known. It has even been claimed the Vatican knew of the Nazi plans concerning the Jewish race.

Also as we already know many of the Nazi command after the war made their way via various routes to Argentina, specifically a town on the Western border of the country called Baranoche. Walk around this quiet town today and you would swear you were in a mountain village in the heart of Germany.

The architecture, most of the street names and most of the signs are all German. The café sells mainly German foods whilst the local bar is most definitely a beer cellar of sorts.

However looking in to this more you see that in order to escape Germany and execution at the hands of the Allied Forces, many of the Nazi command needed help to escape. Luckily for the Nazi's they had a very powerful ally, the Roman Catholic Church

Just inside the Italian border is the town of Tyrol. Nazi's were able to go to a particular church in the town that was sympathetic to the Nazi cause and having suddenly finding God and getting baptised could, with the help of the Red Cross, get a completely new identity and papers to match.

Thus they could then travel without question, without challenge to anywhere in the world, anywhere that is nowhere near prosecution.

All with the help of the Roman Catholic Church and the blessing of the Pope.

Better the Devil you know?

So nowhere near the levels of death they wanted or set out to achieve but still 400 murders in the name of revenge.

Does this act alongside many other probable unknown murders by the group make them justified in their actions? Does it make them criminals or givers of justice?

I know and agree that many of the points I make probably the rants of an atheistic middle aged man but, I am trying to explain, I am attempting to argue that we do not need to believe in an entity that I believe, does not exist.

The Jews were persecuted for being Jewish - a religion
The Catholics murdered people who didn't conform to their – religion
Islamic State murder because they believe they are justified due to – their religion
Closer to home in Northern Ireland the Catholics fought with Protestants – both religions
Years ago people were burned or crucified or fed to a hungry lion because the God or Idol they worshipped wasn't the same as their captures.

Everyone one of us on this planet has a heart, a brain and lungs and everything that puts us together to make this blob we call humanity. There is not one man or woman on this planet that is better at being a human than the person next to them.
    My best friend Simon has a step-son who has Cerebral palsy, does this lesson him as a man, no, he has a wicked sense of humour, he is always looking for the care workers who call because they are mostly pretty young girls that get his heartbeat racing. Does the fact that he cannot learn as others and absorb information, as others can do, stop him from believing in God? On the day of judgement, if there is ever to be one, would every human being in the world today with a learning difficulty, who is unable to follow any sort of faith, would they be turned away from God?

Diary 7

We are now into January 2023. a new year and yet still pain. My pain is getting worse every day. The nerve damage in my spine is making it increasingly difficult to do even the most menial of tasks. My left arm is in pain constantly and my right hip and left knee seem to be giving up as a team. My asthma is also getting worse. I am trying to keep on going, to keep working and to keep some sort of life. I'm 54 years old, too young to give up. The real worry for me however is my mental health. I am increasingly trying so hard to keep on smiling, keep on being the joker, but every day I feel as if I am being dragged deeper and deeper into a pit of self pity and loathing, There never appears to be any good news any more, anywhere or from anyone.

Recent years we have been through all sorts of trauma's including, Covid which it looks like is making a comeback, the Russian invasion of Ukraine which is just becoming more and more of a threat to the rest of us every day due to Putin and his idiotic ideals. Then, perhaps the most embarrassing, annoying and totally unnecessary, the Royal spat between Diana's sons. She would be so ashamed, the world and it's morality is broken.

- My Opinion

With everything going on in the world today it's no wonder the very chance to claim a loving and peaceful life must be engraved on everyone's mind. Religion, no matter which one, has had a resurgence in the world, especially, since the Covid-19 pandemic. Any and every type of escapism is readily sought after and accepted.

It doesn't matter if it is a legal or illegal high, people are just looking for something to take their minds off the lives our governments have created for us.

The war in the Ukraine shows no signs of ending and to make matters worse the tensions between Russia, USA, China and here in the UK are escalating on a daily basis. Will it be the leaders of these countries that suffer? NO! It will be the people who work hard every day to feed their families, the people who worry about the size of every pay packet and how far they can may it stretch to keep going until the next one. There is no bank of God or any other religious entity taking away fears of everyday folk, every day! No golden umbrella stopping bombs and missiles from destroying lives, buildings and history.

If you have actually read all the way through and you actually found what I have written interesting, good, I'm glad. Of course in this work I hopefully have made it obvious that the opinions are mine, and mine alone. The facts, names and dates I have researched on the world wide web. Again, it may be I have read something with only one view in mind and so taken from the work what I want to read, rather than what is meant. I don't know? That is the point surely!!

Years before technology and sciences of any bias became a norm in the world, the word given to an avid listener was the word of God. Which God is up to you. Religious leaders from all around the world could become rich, powerful and feared by those people listening for a sign of better things to come. Just look at such orders as the Knights Templar. A group of religious knights set up to uphold the word of God in very turbulent times, and, for many years what could be called the richest bank in the world. The Templars controlled the money and therefore how people lived.

The most powerful entities in the world for literally thousands of years were governed by a church of one kind or another.

I have read hundreds of pieces of work about religion, about holy wars and how religion has controlled so many for so long. I have tried so hard to understand why people have allowed themselves to be controlled by an invisible entity. I can't!

I would love to be able to understand what makes a person, such as my own mother, fully commit themselves to believe in and follow a God? If you believe in God what makes you believe? What are the proof's that you can physically see or experience that convince you an entity or person you cannot see, cannot hear and cannot physically touch is real? The only real evidence is a written piece of literature from thousands of years ago!

"If the written work from eon's ago is so powerful how come we don't prey to, or, worship mermaids or the Cyclops or any of the mythical creatures that were written about? "

A pointless question requiring an even more obscure, if not polite, answer I know, but, isn't that what followers of any of the faiths are doing?

I have explained in this book that my mental health is on a downward spiral which at the moment I am struggling to get off. I have suffered from severe depression for many, many years, as did my mother. Yet as long as she had her cigarettes, her cups of black coffee and the occasional cheese sandwich, her faith kept her going.

I look at every religious group in the world and all I can see is the pain and suffering that it bestows upon its followers. People live their lives with very little concern for the families around them and the way they live, as long as they look 'proper and respectful' in the eyes of the church then they are happy and content.

'Church Snobbery' was a definite party piece in the church my mother went to. The best hats, the best dresses and of course who was in the Pastors little elite circle?

The Angels now have Kalashnikovs

The first time that we fought it was against the Angels
Next time we fought it was way down there in hell
The third time in war it was for all mankind
But that time my Lord it didn't go so well

Next time in battle the Devil held his pitchfork high
With our shield's to protect us, for our children we will die
There is a fifth time for fighting but we have no chance
The devils are now mocking us and advancing with a dance

We fight against the Angels who threw away mankind
We sacrifice our homes and life so a promise for peace will bind
We reach the stars and galaxies in ships that are made from gold
No one believes in our battles or the stories that are told

From pyramids to MP3's there are challenges in our time
Yet still there is a holy war where ignorance is the crime

So many people, so many thoughts but no one seeks the answer
So many men, women and a child can't believe in ever after.

A wing is cut and a horn is burnt and bodies fall from the sky
And caught once more in a religious war mankind just sits and cries
For not every Angel has a wing not every Devil is red
Sometimes the biggest terror of them all is the misery in your head

Time has lapsed and rivers have run of blood turned into wine
Never has there been a time as now when hope is deemed a crime
The Angels now have Kalashnikov's and the Devils they have bombs
And all man can do is sit and pray looking for what went wrong

The greatest threat on Earth today is man wiping away his brother
Of darkened skin or slanted eyes we are all from Father and Mother
In time it won't matter from where or from whom you are from
As long as you live with humility, not longing for a bomb

But still the Angels fight with man and the Devil shout's out loud
"Why destroy the toys I have, the Angels are devils on a cloud?"
Through sands of time man has built, kingdoms, cities and more
Yet the river that runs through all mankind has made mankind a whore

Whilst cities burn and babies die leaders eat with golden pitched forks
As long as the bombs don't get them, as long as money talks
As long as the people take the brunt of religious men and their guilt
And every leader sleeps well at night, there's no conscience under a quilt

We don't see the miracles now, or the horns or the Angels wings
We only see the hatred and the envy for polished things
So what I say now I say out loud never to be said again
With so much religion in this world it is safer in the lion's den.

There are so many prophets and Gods and bibles that no one has time to read
There are so many reasons and excuses they give for watching the children bleed
Angels will fight and devils will play and each will have their turn   It
is obvious now as someone once said "Some men just want to watch the world burn"

One way I have dealt with my depression was drinking heavily. This of course was and is, neither healthy nor financially astute. After speaking to my GP at that time, she suggested I visited Kaleidoscope. A poor mans version of Alcoholics Anonymous I think? The guy I got to see there was "Ben", a gentle soul, probably late thirties or early forties, and with an uncanny resemblance to Liam Gallagher.

Most definitely a hippy of sorts, Ben brought out memories and feelings I never knew I had. This is where my distrust of religion emerged with great gusto. I had been an angry atheist ever since my mothers death in 2005, but now all of the feelings I was fighting with all of a sudden were making sense.

Writing this book has taken roughly 4 years to complete. Throughout I have tried so hard to make sense of what is going on both in my head and the world. It is May 2023 and this weekend the new King of Great Britain and Northern Ireland, Charles III, will be crowned. All the news can talk about is the various groups who are planning to protest the royalty, it's pomp and splendour!

The whole day of the coronation is centred around the word of God being bestowed upon Charles in order to do his duty as King. The money involved in the day is bound to be stupendously high. I wonder how much Westminster Abbey is actually charging for the event? The new breed of Royals to a certain level I agree with. The Royal family does bring tourism into the UK, therefore, money!

Conclusion and Reference

I still can't see how a religious entity can have so much affect on the people of the world, I agree both positively as well as negatively? There is so much hatred in the world much of which is promoted by one form of religion or another.

I repeat what I said earlier:

"Put me in a room with a group of Holy leaders from various faiths and ask them to convince me that the God they worship is real?!"

In writing this I have listened to people I know and trust. I have read books and I watched documentaries both online and on television.

Reference:
     Holy Blood and the Holy Grail by Michael Baigent, Richard Leigh and Henry Lincoln.
     The Holy Bible by various contributors.
     Various and many opinions and television programs.

My beloved Mother, Pauline Aleman, who gave everything to her God and her Church and for what?

For Olivia

For Jo

For Booboo

Printed in Great Britain
by Amazon

32050465R00044